Common Core Lessons

Text-Based
Writing Nonfiction

Grade 6

The following photos were provided through Shutterstock.com and are protected by copyright:
Lauren Jade Goudie (page 14); clivewa (page 15); ramcreations, studio, Vereshchagin Dmitry, risteski goce, MO_SES, Nik Merkulov (page 24); Alex Staroseltsev (page 25); Sergey Furtaev (page 34); auremar (page 44); Steve Byland (page 64); 3drenderings (page 65); ArtisticPhoto (page 74); Mircea BEZERGHEANU, Vacclav (page 104); Eric Isselee, Leksele (page 105); studioVin (page 124)

The remaining photos were provided by the organizations and individuals listed below and are also protected by copyright:
Bloemmie29 (page 55); Koa Halpern (pages 84, 85); Victor David Brenner, Lyndall Bass (page 114)

Writing: Carrie Gwynne
Editorial Development: Renee Biermann
Lisa Vitarisi Mathews
Copy Editing: Cathy Harber
Art Direction: Cheryl Puckett
Art Management: Kathy Kopp
Cover Design: Yuki Meyer
Cover Illustration: Chris Vallo
Design/Production: Susan Lovell
Jessica Onken

EMC 6036

Visit
teaching-standards.com
to view a correlation
of this book.
This is a free service.

**Correlated to State and
Common Core State Standards**

**Congratulations on your purchase of some of the
finest teaching materials in the world.**

*Photocopying the pages in this book
is permitted for <u>single-classroom use only</u>.
Making photocopies for additional classes
or schools is prohibited.*

For information about other Evan-Moor products, call 1-800-777-4362,
fax 1-800-777-4332, or visit our Web site, www.evan-moor.com.
Entire contents © 2014 EVAN-MOOR CORP.
18 Lower Ragsdale Drive, Monterey, CA 93940-5746. Printed in USA.

CPSIA: Printed by McNaughton & Gunn, Saline, MI USA.[2/2015]

Contents

Introduction

Informative/Explanatory Writing Prompts

Opinion/Argument Writing Prompts

What's in Every Unit?

Resource pages outline lesson objectives and provide instructional guidance.

The reading level helps identify appropriate texts.

Lesson objectives and content-area concepts are indicated.

Common Core State Standards correlations are located in each unit for easy reference.

A suggested learning path helps you pace the lesson.

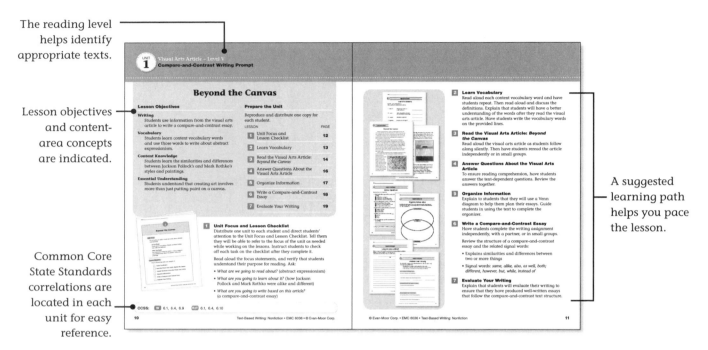

Student pages provide unit focus, organizational tools, nonfiction content, and skills practice.

1 Unit Focus and Lesson Checklist

The Unit Focus provides a purpose for reading.

The Lesson Checklist guides students through the learning path.

2 Vocabulary

A dictionary introduces content words and provides definitions.

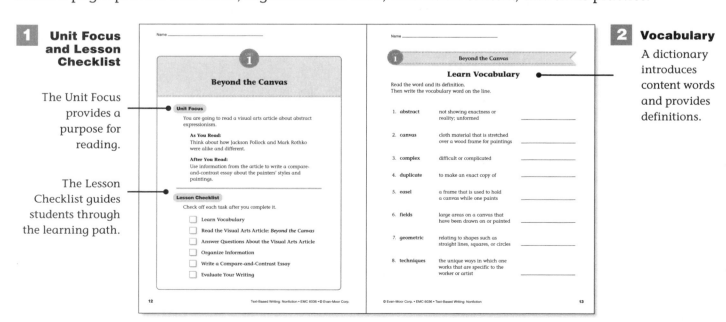

3 **Nonfiction Article**

A two-page article introduces a content-area topic and provides details.

Illustrations and graphics provide additional information and context.

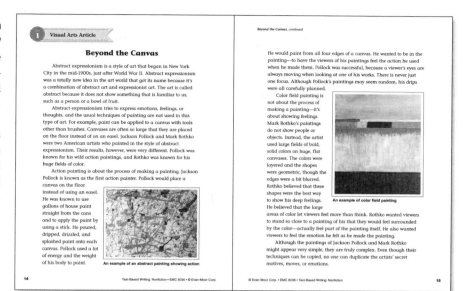

Visual Arts Article

Beyond the Canvas

Abstract expressionism is a style of art that began in New York City in the mid-1900s, just after World War II. Abstract expressionism was a totally new idea in the art world that got its name because it's a combination of abstract art and expressionist art. The art is called abstract because it does not show something that is familiar to us, such as a person or a bowl of fruit.

Abstract expressionism tries to express emotions, feelings, or thoughts, and the usual techniques of painting are not used in this type of art. For example, paint can be applied to a canvas with tools other than brushes. Canvases are often so large that they are placed on the floor instead of on an easel. Jackson Pollock and Mark Rothko were two American artists who painted in the style of abstract expressionism. Their results, however, were very different. Pollock was known for his wild action paintings, and Rothko was known for his huge fields of color.

Action painting is about the process of making a painting. Jackson Pollock is known as the first action painter. Pollock would place a canvas on the floor instead of using an easel. He was known to use gallons of house paint straight from the cans and to apply the paint by using a stick. He poured, dripped, drizzled, and splashed paint onto each canvas. Pollock used a lot of energy and the weight of his body to paint.

An example of an abstract painting showing action

He would paint from all four edges of a canvas. He wanted to be in the painting—to have the viewers of his paintings feel the action he used when he made them. Pollock was successful, because a viewer's eyes are always moving when looking at one of his works. There is never just one focus. Although Pollock's paintings may seem random, his drips were all carefully planned.

Color field painting is not about the process of making a painting—it's about showing feelings. Mark Rothko's paintings do not show people or objects. Instead, the artist used large fields of bold, solid colors on huge, flat canvases. The colors were layered and the shapes were geometric, though the edges were a bit blurred. Rothko believed that these shapes were the best way to show his deep feelings. He believed that the large areas of color let viewers feel more than think. Rothko wanted viewers to stand so close to a painting of his that they would feel surrounded by the color—actually feel part of the painting itself. He also wanted viewers to feel the emotion he felt as he made the painting.

An example of color field painting

Although the paintings of Jackson Pollock and Mark Rothko might appear very simple, they are truly complex. Even though their techniques can be copied, no one can duplicate the artists' secret motives, moves, or emotions.

4 **Comprehension Questions**

Text-based questions appear in multiple-choice and constructed-response formats.

5 **Graphic Organizer**

A graphic organizer helps students organize information from the article to plan their writing.

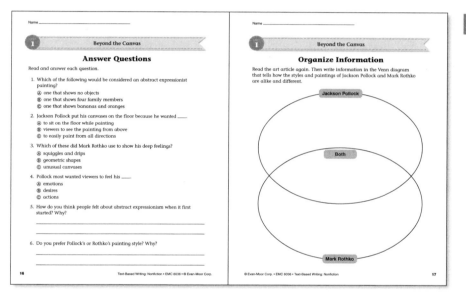

Name _____

Beyond the Canvas

Answer Questions

Read and answer each question.

1. Which of the following would be considered an abstract expressionist painting?
   A one that shows no objects
   B one that shows four family members
   C one that shows bananas and oranges

2. Jackson Pollock put his canvases on the floor because he wanted _____
   A to sit on the floor while painting
   B viewers to see the painting from above
   C to easily paint from all directions

3. Which of these did Mark Rothko use to show his deep feelings?
   A squiggles and drips
   B geometric shapes
   C unusual canvases

4. Pollock most wanted viewers to feel his _____
   A emotions
   B desires
   C actions

5. How do you think people felt about abstract expressionism when it first started? Why?
   _____
   _____

6. Do you prefer Pollock's or Rothko's painting style? Why?
   _____
   _____

Name _____

Beyond the Canvas

Organize Information

Read the art article again. Then write information in the Venn diagram that tells how the styles and paintings of Jackson Pollock and Mark Rothko are alike and different.

Jackson Pollock

Both

Mark Rothko

6 **Writing Prompt**

A text-based writing prompt helps students synthesize what they've learned.

7 **Writing Evaluation**

A review of nonfiction writing structures guides students in evaluating their essay.

Name _____

Beyond the Canvas

Compare and Contrast

Write a compare-and-contrast essay about **how Jackson Pollock and Mark Rothko were alike and different.** Describe their styles and paintings. Use information from your Venn diagram and the art article.

Title _____

Name _____

Beyond the Canvas

Evaluate Your Writing

Read about the compare-and-contrast text structure. Then use your essay to complete the activity below.

A text that has a **compare-and-contrast** structure makes comparisons, or describes similarities between two or more things. It also contrasts, or describes how these things are different.

The reason for writing is clear.

My essay compared and contrasted:
_____

I used these compare-and-contrast signal words:
_____ _____ _____

I provided details that support the topic.

I included these detail sentences:
1. _____
2. _____

My paragraphs have a clear focus.

My opening sentence for the first paragraph is:
_____

My closing sentence for the first paragraph is:
_____

Correlations:
Common Core State Standards

	Units					
	1	**2**	**3**	**4**	**5**	**6**
W **Writing Standards for Grade 6**	Beyond the Canvas	Finding Your Way	The Benefits of Laughter	Motion Sickness	Jennifer Rodriguez	Fancy Fliers
Text Types and Purposes						
6.1 Write arguments to support claims with clear reasons and relevant evidence. **a.** Introduce claim(s) and organize the reasons and evidence clearly. **b.** Support claim(s) with clear reasons and relevant evidence, using credible sources and demonstrating an understanding of the topic or text.	●	●	●	●	●	●
6.2 Write informative/explanatory texts to examine a topic and convey ideas, concepts, and information through the selection, organization, and analysis of relevant content.						
Production and Distribution of Writing						
6.4 Produce clear and coherent writing in which the development, organization, and style are appropriate to task, purpose, and audience. (Grade-specific expectations for writing types are defined in standards 1 and 2 above.)	●	●	●	●	●	●
Research to Build and Present Knowledge						
6.9 Draw evidence from literary or informational texts to support analysis, reflection, and research.	●	●	●	●	●	●
RIT **Reading Standards for Informational Text, Grade 6**						
Key Ideas and Details						
6.1 Cite textual evidence to support analysis of what the text says explicitly as well as inferences drawn from the text.	●	●	●	●	●	●
Craft and Structure						
6.4 Determine the meaning of words and phrases as they are used in a text, including figurative, connotative, and technical meanings.	●	●	●	●	●	●
Range of Reading and Level of Text Complexity						
6.10 By the end of year, read and comprehend literary nonfiction in the grades 6–8 text complexity band proficiently, with scaffolding as needed at the high end of the range.	●	●	●	●	●	●

Units						
7	8	9	10	11	12	**W** Writing Standards for Grade 6
The United Nations	Koa Halpern	Safety First	Bioengineering	A Penny's Worth	The Science of Flavor	
						Text Types and Purposes
●						**6.1** Write arguments to support claims with clear reasons and relevant evidence. **a.** Introduce claim(s) and organize the reasons and evidence clearly. **b.** Support claim(s) with clear reasons and relevant evidence, using credible sources and demonstrating an understanding of the topic or text.
	●	●	●	●	●	**6.2** Write informative/explanatory texts to examine a topic and convey ideas, concepts, and information through the selection, organization, and analysis of relevant content.
						Production and Distribution of Writing
●	●	●	●	●	●	**6.4** Produce clear and coherent writing in which the development, organization, and style are appropriate to task, purpose, and audience. (Grade-specific expectations for writing types are defined in standards 1 and 2 above.)
						Research to Build and Present Knowledge
●	●	●	●	●	●	**6.9** Draw evidence from literary or informational texts to support analysis, reflection, and research.

7	8	9	10	11	12	**RIT** Reading Standards for Informational Text, Grade 6
						Key Ideas and Details
●	●	●	●	●	●	**6.1** Cite textual evidence to support analysis of what the text says explicitly as well as inferences drawn from the text.
						Craft and Structure
●	●	●	●	●	●	**6.4** Determine the meaning of words and phrases as they are used in a text, including figurative, connotative, and technical meanings.
						Range of Reading and Level of Text Complexity
●	●	●	●	●	●	**6.10** By the end of year, read and comprehend literary nonfiction in the grades 6–8 text complexity band proficiently, with scaffolding as needed at the high end of the range.

Correlations:
Texas Essential Knowledge and Skills

110.18 English Language Arts and Reading, Grade 6	Units				
	1	2	3	4	5
	Beyond the Canvas	Finding Your Way	The Benefits of Laughter	Motion Sickness	Jennifer Rodriguez
Writing					
(14) Writing/Writing Process. Students use elements of the writing process (planning, drafting, revising, editing, and publishing) to compose text. Students are expected to:	●	●	●	●	●
(B) develop drafts by choosing an appropriate organizational strategy (e.g., sequence of events, cause-effect, compare-contrast) and building on ideas to create a focused, organized, and coherent piece of writing.	●	●	●	●	●
(17) Writing/Expository and Procedural Texts. Students write expository and procedural or work-related texts to communicate ideas and information to specific audiences for specific purposes. Students are expected to:	●	●	●	●	●
(C) write responses to literary or expository texts and provide evidence from the text to demonstrate understanding.	●	●	●	●	●
(18) Writing/Persuasive Texts. Students write persuasive texts to influence the attitudes or actions of a specific audience on specific issues. Students are expected to write persuasive essays for appropriate audiences that establish a position and include sound reasoning, detailed and relevant evidence, and consideration of alternatives.					
Reading					
(10) Reading/Comprehension of Informational Text/ Expository Text. Students analyze, make inferences, and draw conclusions about expository text and provide evidence from text to support their understanding. Students are expected to:	●	●	●	●	●
(A) summarize the main ideas and supporting details in text, demonstrating an understanding that a summary does not include opinions;	●	●	●	●	●
(B) explain whether facts included in an argument are used for or against an issue; and		●			
(C) explain how different organizational patterns (e.g., proposition-and-support, problem-and-solution) develop the main idea and the author's viewpoint.	●	●	●	●	●
(12) Reading/Comprehension of Informational Text/ Procedural Texts. Students understand how to glean and use information in procedural texts and documents. Students are expected to:	●		●	●	
(B) interpret factual, quantitative, or technical information presented in maps, charts, illustrations, graphs, timelines, tables, and diagrams.	●	●	●	●	●

Units						
6	7	8	9	10	11	12
Fancy Fliers	The United Nations	Koa Halpern	Safety First	Bioengineering	A Penny's Worth	The Science of Flavor
●	●	●	●	●	●	●
●	●	●	●	●	●	●
●	●					
●	●	●	●	●	●	●
		●	●	●	●	●
●	●	●	●	●	●	●
●	●	●	●	●	●	●
					●	
●	●	●	●	●	●	●
			●	●		●
●	●	●	●	●	●	●

Beyond the Canvas

Lesson Objectives

Writing
Students use information from the visual arts article to write a compare-and-contrast essay.

Vocabulary
Students learn content vocabulary words and use those words to write about abstract expressionism.

Content Knowledge
Students learn the similarities and differences between Jackson Pollock's and Mark Rothko's styles and paintings.

Essential Understanding
Students understand that creating art involves more than just putting paint on a canvas.

Prepare the Unit

Reproduce and distribute one copy for each student.

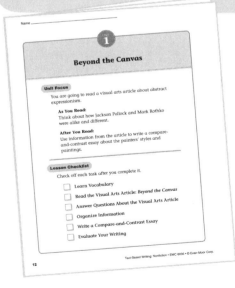

Name _____

1

Beyond the Canvas

Unit Focus
You are going to read a visual arts article about abstract expressionism.

As You Read:
Think about how Jackson Pollock and Mark Rothko were alike and different.

After You Read:
Use information from the article to write a compare-and-contrast essay about the painters' styles and paintings.

Lesson Checklist
Check off each task after you complete it.
☐ Learn Vocabulary
☐ Read the Visual Arts Article: *Beyond the Canvas*
☐ Answer Questions About the Visual Arts Article
☐ Organize Information
☐ Write a Compare-and-Contrast Essay
☐ Evaluate Your Writing

Text-Based Writing: Nonfiction • EMC 6036 • © Evan-Moor Corp.

12

1 ## Unit Focus and Lesson Checklist

Distribute one unit to each student and direct students' attention to the Unit Focus and Lesson Checklist. Tell them they will be able to refer to the focus of the unit as needed while working on the lessons. Instruct students to check off each task on the checklist after they complete it.

Read aloud the focus statements, and verify that students understand their purpose for reading. Ask:

- *What are we going to read about?* (abstract expressionism)

- *What are you going to learn about it?* (how Jackson Pollock and Mark Rothko were alike and different)

- *What are you going to write based on this article?* (a compare-and-contrast essay)

CCSS: **W** 6.1, 6.4, 6.9   **RIT** 6.1, 6.4, 6.10

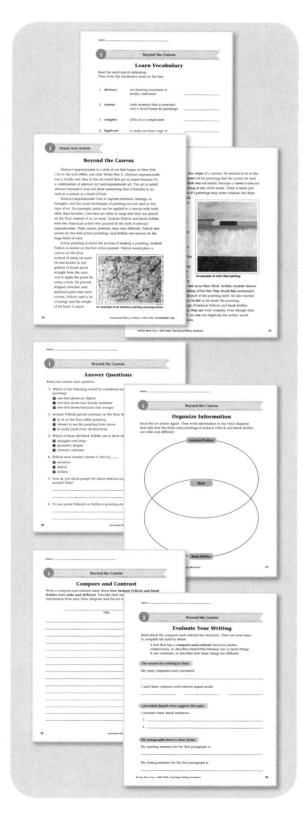

2 Learn Vocabulary

Read aloud each content vocabulary word and have students repeat. Then read aloud and discuss the definitions. Explain that students will have a better understanding of the words after they read the visual arts article. Have students write the vocabulary words on the provided lines.

3 Read the Visual Arts Article: *Beyond the Canvas*

Read aloud the visual arts article as students follow along silently. Then have students reread the article independently or in small groups.

4 Answer Questions About the Visual Arts Article

To ensure reading comprehension, have students answer the text-dependent questions. Review the answers together.

5 Organize Information

Explain to students that they will use a Venn diagram to help them plan their essays. Guide students in using the text to complete the organizer.

6 Write a Compare-and-Contrast Essay

Have students complete the writing assignment independently, with a partner, or in small groups.

Review the structure of a compare-and-contrast essay and the related signal words:

- Explains similarities and differences between two or more things

- Signal words: *same, alike, also, as well, both; different, however, but, while, instead of*

7 Evaluate Your Writing

Explain that students will evaluate their writing to ensure that they have produced well-written essays that follow the compare-and-contrast text structure.

Beyond the Canvas

Unit Focus

You are going to read a visual arts article about abstract expressionism.

As You Read:

Think about how Jackson Pollock and Mark Rothko were alike and different.

After You Read:

Use information from the article to write a compare-and-contrast essay about the painters' styles and paintings.

Lesson Checklist

Check off each task after you complete it.

- [ ] **Learn Vocabulary**
- [ ] **Read the Visual Arts Article:** *Beyond the Canvas*
- [ ] **Answer Questions About the Visual Arts Article**
- [ ] **Organize Information**
- [ ] **Write a Compare-and-Contrast Essay**
- [ ] **Evaluate Your Writing**

Name _____

UNIT
1

Beyond the Canvas

Learn Vocabulary

Read the word and its definition.
Then write the vocabulary word on the line.

1. **abstract**   not showing exactness or
                      reality; unformed   _____

2. **canvas**   cloth material that is stretched
                      over a wood frame for paintings   _____

3. **complex**   difficult or complicated   _____

4. **duplicate**   to make an exact copy of   _____

5. **easel**   a frame that is used to hold
                      a canvas while one paints   _____

6. **fields**   large areas on a canvas that
                      have been drawn on or painted   _____

7. **geometric**   relating to shapes such as
                      straight lines, squares, or circles _____

8. **techniques**   the unique ways in which one
                      works that are specific to the
                      worker or artist   _____

Beyond the Canvas

Abstract expressionism is a style of art that began in New York City in the mid-1900s, just after World War II. Abstract expressionism was a totally new idea in the art world that got its name because it's a combination of abstract art and expressionist art. The art is called abstract because it does not show something that is familiar to us, such as a person or a bowl of fruit.

Abstract expressionism tries to express emotions, feelings, or thoughts, and the usual techniques of painting are not used in this type of art. For example, paint can be applied to a canvas with tools other than brushes. Canvases are often so large that they are placed on the floor instead of on an easel. Jackson Pollock and Mark Rothko were two American artists who painted in the style of abstract expressionism. Their results, however, were very different. Pollock was known for his wild action paintings, and Rothko was known for his huge fields of color.

Action painting is about the process of making a painting. Jackson Pollock is known as the first action painter. Pollock would place a canvas on the floor instead of using an easel. He was known to use gallons of house paint straight from the cans and to apply the paint by using a stick. He poured, dripped, drizzled, and splashed paint onto each canvas. Pollock used a lot of energy and the weight of his body to paint.

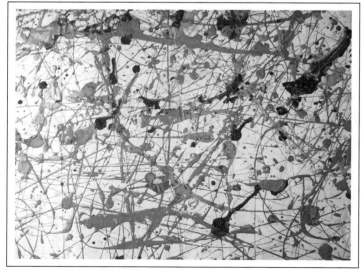

An example of an abstract painting showing action

He would paint from all four edges of a canvas. He wanted to be in the painting—to have the viewers of his paintings feel the action he used when he made them. Pollock was successful, because a viewer's eyes are always moving when looking at one of his works. There is never just one focus. Although Pollock's paintings may seem random, his drips were all carefully planned.

Color field painting is not about the process of making a painting—it's about showing feelings. Mark Rothko's paintings do not show people or objects. Instead, the artist used large fields of bold, solid colors on huge, flat canvases. The colors were layered and the shapes were geometric, though the edges were a bit blurred. Rothko believed that these shapes were the best way to show his deep feelings. He believed that the large areas of color let viewers feel more than think. Rothko wanted viewers to stand so close to a painting of his that they would feel surrounded by the color—actually feel part of the painting itself. He also wanted viewers to feel the emotion he felt as he made the painting.

An example of color field painting

Although the paintings of Jackson Pollock and Mark Rothko might appear very simple, they are truly complex. Even though their techniques can be copied, no one can duplicate the artists' secret motives, moves, or emotions.

UNIT 1

Beyond the Canvas

Answer Questions

Read and answer each question.

1. Which of the following would be considered an abstract expressionist painting?

   Ⓐ one that shows no objects

   Ⓑ one that shows four family members

   Ⓒ one that shows bananas and oranges

2. Jackson Pollock put his canvases on the floor because he wanted _____.

   Ⓐ to sit on the floor while painting

   Ⓑ viewers to see the painting from above

   Ⓒ to easily paint from all directions

3. Which of these did Mark Rothko use to show his deep feelings?

   Ⓐ squiggles and drips

   Ⓑ geometric shapes

   Ⓒ unusual canvases

4. Pollock most wanted viewers to feel his _____.

   Ⓐ emotions

   Ⓑ desires

   Ⓒ actions

5. How do you think people felt about abstract expressionism when it first started? Why?

   _____

   _____

6. Do you prefer Pollock's or Rothko's painting style? Why?

   _____

   _____

Text-Based Writing: Nonfiction • EMC 6036 • © Evan-Moor Corp.

Organize Information

Read the art article again. Then write information in the Venn diagram that tells how the styles and paintings of Jackson Pollock and Mark Rothko are alike and different.

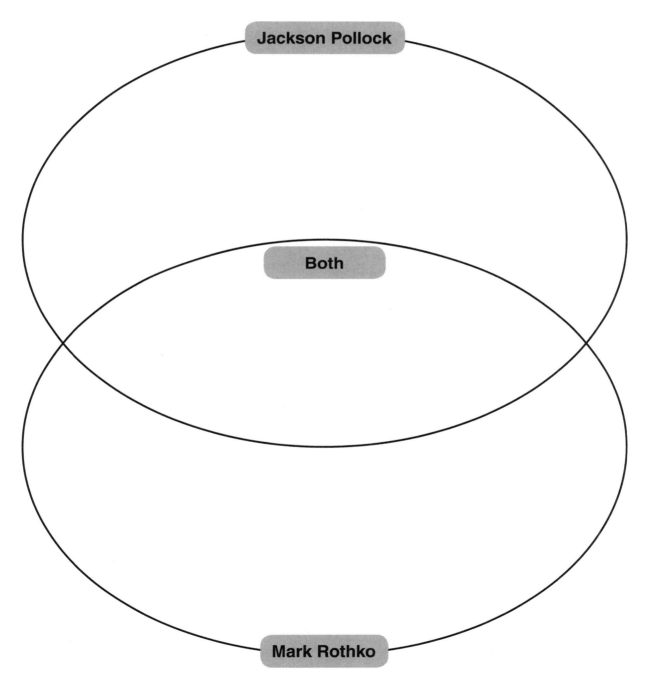

Jackson Pollock

Both

Mark Rothko

Beyond the Canvas

Compare and Contrast

Write a compare-and-contrast essay about **how Jackson Pollock and Mark Rothko were alike and different**. Describe their styles and paintings. Use information from your Venn diagram and the art article.

_____

Title

_____

_____

_____

_____

_____

_____

_____

_____

_____

_____

_____

_____

_____

Name _____

Evaluate Your Writing

Read about the compare-and-contrast text structure. Then use your essay to complete the activity below.

> A text that has a **compare-and-contrast** structure makes comparisons, or describes similarities between two or more things. It also contrasts, or describes how these things are different.

The reason for writing is clear.

My essay compared and contrasted:

_____

I used these compare-and-contrast signal words:

_____   _____   _____

I provided details that support the topic.

I included these detail sentences:

1. _____

2. _____

My paragraphs have a clear focus.

My opening sentence for the first paragraph is:

_____

My closing sentence for the first paragraph is:

_____

Finding Your Way

Lesson Objectives

Writing
Students use information from the science article to write a compare-and-contrast essay.

Vocabulary
Students learn content vocabulary words and use those words to write about the similarities and differences between navigational tools.

Content Knowledge
Students learn the functions and pros and cons of using compasses, maps, and a GPS.

Essential Understanding
Students understand that a GPS is very useful, but that compasses and maps can still be beneficial tools.

Prepare the Unit

Reproduce and distribute one copy for each student.

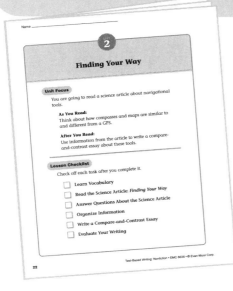

1 Unit Focus and Lesson Checklist

Distribute one unit to each student and direct students' attention to the Unit Focus and Lesson Checklist. Tell them they will be able to refer to the focus of the unit as needed while working on the lessons. Instruct students to check off each task on the checklist after they complete it.

Read aloud the focus statements, and verify that students understand their purpose for reading. Ask:

- *What are we going to read about?* (navigational tools)

- *What are you going to learn about them?* (how they are alike and different)

- *What are you going to write based on this article?* (a compare-and-contrast essay)

CCSS: 6.1, 6.4, 6.9   6.1, 6.4, 6.10

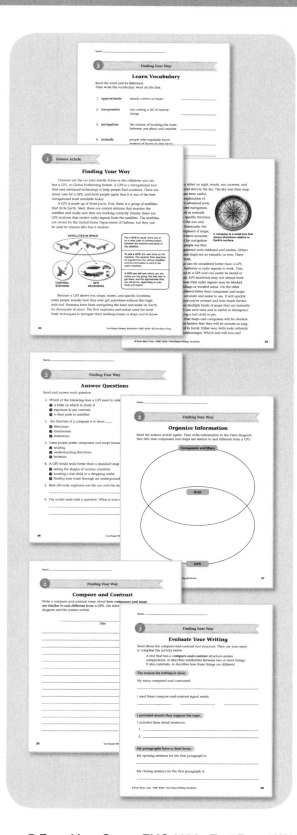

2 Learn Vocabulary

Read aloud each content vocabulary word and have students repeat. Then read aloud and discuss the definitions. Explain that students will have a better understanding of the words after they read the science article. Have students write the vocabulary words on the provided lines.

3 Read the Science Article: *Finding Your Way*

Read aloud the science article as students follow along silently. Then have students reread the article independently or in small groups.

4 Answer Questions About the Science Article

To ensure reading comprehension, have students answer the text-dependent questions. Review the answers together.

5 Organize Information

Explain to students that they will use a Venn diagram to help them plan their essays. Guide students in using the text to complete the organizer.

6 Write a Compare-and-Contrast Essay

Have students complete the writing assignment independently, with a partner, or in small groups.

Review the structure of a compare-and-contrast essay and the related signal words:

- Explains similarities and differences between two or more things

- Signal words: *same, alike, also, as well, both; different, however, but, while, instead of*

7 Evaluate Your Writing

Explain that students will evaluate their writing to ensure that they have produced well-written essays that follow the compare-and-contrast text structure.

UNIT
2

Finding Your Way

Unit Focus

You are going to read a science article about navigational tools.

As You Read:

Think about how compasses and maps are similar to and different from a GPS.

After You Read:

Use information from the article to write a compare-and-contrast essay about these tools.

Lesson Checklist

Check off each task after you complete it.

- [ ] **Learn Vocabulary**
- [ ] **Read the Science Article:** *Finding Your Way*
- [ ] **Answer Questions About the Science Article**
- [ ] **Organize Information**
- [ ] **Write a Compare-and-Contrast Essay**
- [ ] **Evaluate Your Writing**

Learn Vocabulary

Read the word and its definition.
Then write the vocabulary word on the line.

1. **approximate**   nearly correct or exact   _____

2. **inexpensive**   not costing a lot of money; cheap   _____

3. **navigation**   the science of locating the route between one place and another   _____

4. **nomads**   people who regularly move instead of living in one place   _____

5. **obsolete**   no longer useful or available   _____

6. **obstacles**   physical objects in the way of one's path   _____

7. **revolutionized**   made vastly different; changed completely in a beneficial way   _____

8. **satellites**   machines that orbit Earth   _____

9. **sea currents**   strong movements of water in the world's oceans   _____

Finding Your Way

Chances are the car your family drives or the cellphone you use has a GPS, or Global Positioning System. A GPS is a navigational tool that uses advanced technology to help people find locations. There are many uses for a GPS, and most people agree that it is one of the best navigational tools available today.

A GPS is made up of three parts. First, there is a group of satellites that circle Earth. Next, there are control stations that monitor the satellites and make sure they are working correctly. Finally, there are GPS receivers that receive radio signals from the satellites. The satellites are owned by the United States Department of Defense, but they can be used by anyone who has a receiver.

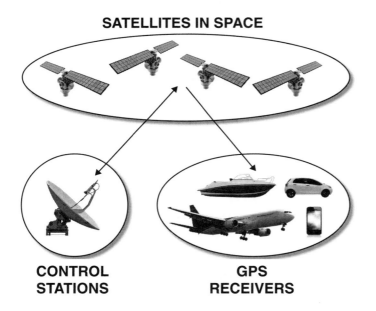

SATELLITES IN SPACE

CONTROL STATIONS

GPS RECEIVERS

For a GPS to work, there has to be a clear path of communication between the receiver and some of the satellites.

To use a GPS, the user turns on the machine. The receiver then searches for signals from the various satellites, and the information is sent to the user's machine.

A GPS can tell you where you are, where you are going, the best way to get there, and the approximate time you will arrive, depending on your route and speed.

Because a GPS shows you maps, routes, and specific locations, some people wonder how they ever got anywhere without this high-tech tool. Humans have been navigating the land and water on Earth for thousands of years. The first explorers and sailors used the most basic techniques to navigate their walking routes or ships and to know their own locations. They relied on sight, winds, sea currents, and the positions of the sun and stars in the sky. The sky was their map.

These basic techniques were useful, but accurate, long-term exploration of our planet required more advanced tools. The compass revolutionized navigation. A compass allowed sailors or nomads to continue moving in a specific direction when bad weather made the sun and the stars difficult to see. Eventually, the compass led to the development of maps, which became more and more accurate. Over time, the tools used for navigation expanded. Today, some people say that

A compass is a small tool that shows directions relative to Earth's surface.

a GPS makes older navigational tools outdated and useless. Others believe that compasses and maps are as valuable as ever. There are valid arguments for both.

Compasses and maps can be considered better than a GPS because they don't need batteries or radio signals to work. They are inexpensive compared to a GPS and can easily be stored or placed on a table for study. GPS machines may not always work in certain locations because their radio signals may be blocked by obstacles such as buildings or wooded areas. On the other hand, a GPS can be considered better than compasses and maps because it may be more accurate and easier to use. It will quickly tell you how much distance you've covered and how much farther you have to go. It also has multiple kinds of maps that are instantly available to users. A GPS can save time and is useful in emergency situations, such as tracking a lost child or pet.

Some people believe that maps and compasses will be obsolete in the future, while others believe that they will be around as long as humans have the need to travel. Either way, both tools certainly have advantages and disadvantages. Which tool will you use?

UNIT 2

Finding Your Way

Answer Questions

Read and answer each question.

1. Which of the following does a GPS need in order to function properly?
   Ⓐ a table on which to study it
   Ⓑ exposure to sea currents
   Ⓒ a clear path to satellites

2. The function of a compass is to show ____.
   Ⓐ directions
   Ⓑ landmasses
   Ⓒ waterways

3. Some people prefer compasses and maps because they do not require ____.
   Ⓐ reading
   Ⓑ understanding directions
   Ⓒ batteries

4. A GPS would work better than a standard map for ____.
   Ⓐ seeing the shapes of various countries
   Ⓑ locating a lost child at a shopping center
   Ⓒ finding your route through an underground cave

5. How did early explorers use the sun and the stars to travel? Explain.

   _____

6. The article ends with a question. What is your answer? Why?

   _____

   _____

Name _____

Organize Information

Read the science article again. Then write information in the Venn diagram that tells how compasses and maps are similar to and different from a GPS.

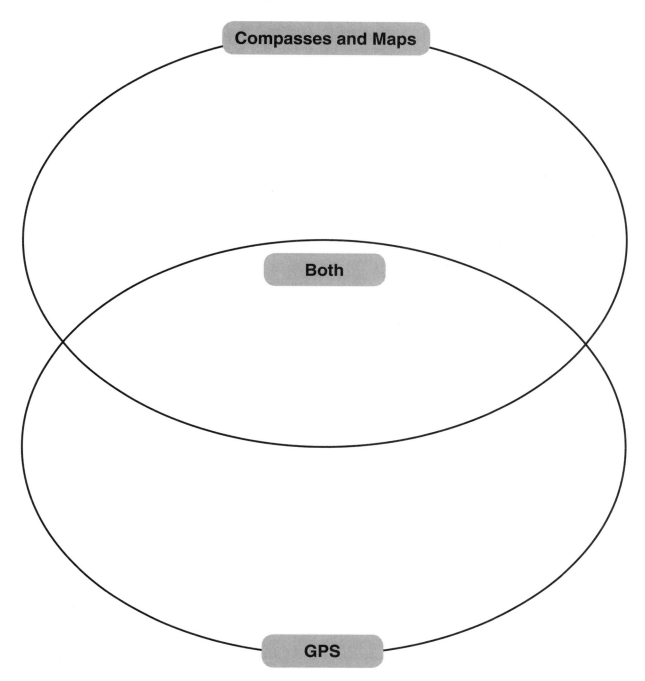

Compasses and Maps

Both

GPS

UNIT 2 ··········· **Finding Your Way** ···········

Compare and Contrast

Write a compare-and-contrast essay about **how compasses and maps are similar to and different from a GPS**. Use information from your Venn diagram and the science article.

_____
Title

_____

_____

_____

_____

_____

_____

_____

_____

_____

_____

_____

_____

_____

UNIT 2 ·

Finding Your Way

Evaluate Your Writing

Read about the compare-and-contrast text structure. Then use your essay to complete the activity below.

> A text that has a **compare-and-contrast** structure makes comparisons, or describes similarities between two or more things. It also contrasts, or describes how these things are different.

The reason for writing is clear.

My essay compared and contrasted:

_____

I used these compare-and-contrast signal words:

_____   _____   _____

I provided details that support the topic.

I included these detail sentences:

1. _____

2. _____

My paragraphs have a clear focus.

My opening sentence for the first paragraph is:

_____

My closing sentence for the first paragraph is:

_____

The Benefits of Laughter

Lesson Objectives

Writing
Students use information from the health article to write a cause-and-effect essay.

Vocabulary
Students learn content vocabulary words and use those words to write about laughter.

Content Knowledge
Students learn about the mental and physical benefits of laughter.

Essential Understanding
Students understand that laughing regularly can help them improve their mental health, physical health, and social lives.

Prepare the Unit

Reproduce and distribute one copy for each student.

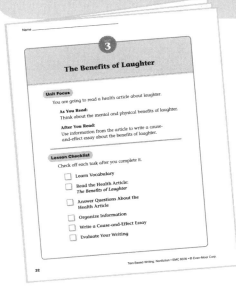

1 Unit Focus and Lesson Checklist

Distribute one unit to each student and direct students' attention to the Unit Focus and Lesson Checklist. Tell them they will be able to refer to the focus of the unit as needed while working on the lessons. Instruct students to check off each task on the checklist after they complete it.

Read aloud the focus statements, and verify that students understand their purpose for reading. Ask:

- *What are we going to read about?* (laughter)

- *What are you going to learn about it?* (the mental and physical benefits)

- *What are you going to write based on this article?* (a cause-and-effect essay)

CCSS: 6.1, 6.4, 6.9   6.1, 6.4, 6.10

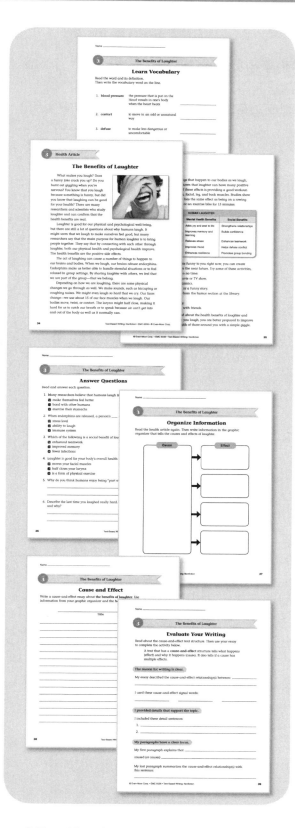

2 Learn Vocabulary

Read aloud each content vocabulary word and have students repeat. Then read aloud and discuss the definitions. Explain that students will have a better understanding of the words after they read the health article. Have students write the vocabulary words on the provided lines.

3 Read the Health Article: *The Benefits of Laughter*

Read aloud the health article as students follow along silently. Then have students reread the article independently or in small groups.

4 Answer Questions About the Health Article

To ensure reading comprehension, have students answer the text-dependent questions. Review the answers together.

5 Organize Information

Explain to students that they will use a cause-and-effect graphic organizer to help them plan their essays. Guide students in using the text to complete the organizer.

6 Write a Cause-and-Effect Essay

Have students complete the writing assignment independently, with a partner, or in small groups.

Review the structure of a cause-and-effect essay and the related signal words:

• Explains what happens (effect) and why it happens (cause)

• Signal words: *because, therefore, so, since, as a result*

7 Evaluate Your Writing

Explain that students will evaluate their writing to ensure that they have produced well-written essays that follow the cause-and-effect text structure.

UNIT
3

The Benefits of Laughter

Unit Focus

You are going to read a health article about laughter.

As You Read:

Think about the mental and physical benefits of laughter.

After You Read:

Use information from the article to write a cause-and-effect essay about the benefits of laughter.

Lesson Checklist

Check off each task after you complete it.

- [ ] **Learn Vocabulary**

- [ ] **Read the Health Article:**
  The Benefits of Laughter

- [ ] **Answer Questions About the Health Article**

- [ ] **Organize Information**

- [ ] **Write a Cause-and-Effect Essay**

- [ ] **Evaluate Your Writing**

Learn Vocabulary

Read the word and its definition.
Then write the vocabulary word on the line.

1. **blood pressure**   the pressure that is put on the
blood vessels in one's body
when the heart beats   _____

2. **contort**   to move in an odd or unnatural
way   _____

3. **defuse**   to make less dangerous or
uncomfortable   _____

4. **endorphins**   natural chemicals in the brain
that make humans feel good
or happy   _____

5. **immunity**   the body's ability to resist
disease   _____

6. **larynx**   the part of the upper throat that
allows humans to speak or make
sounds   _____

7. **psychological**   relating to the mind or thoughts   _____

8. **resilience**   the ability to stay strong or
brave during hard times   _____

The Benefits of Laughter

What makes you laugh? Does a funny joke crack you up? Do you burst out giggling when you're nervous? You know that you laugh because something is funny, but did you know that laughing can be good for your health? There are many researchers and scientists who study laughter and can confirm that the health benefits are real.

Laughter is good for our physical and psychological well-being, but there are still a lot of questions about why humans laugh. It might seem that we laugh to make ourselves feel good, but many researchers say that the main purpose for human laughter is to bring people together. They say that by connecting with each other through laughter, both our physical health and psychological health improve. The health benefits are the positive side effects.

The act of laughing can cause a number of things to happen to our brains and bodies. When we laugh, our brains release endorphins. Endorphins make us better able to handle stressful situations or to feel relaxed in group settings. By sharing laughter with others, we feel that we are part of the group—that we belong.

Depending on how we are laughing, there are some physical changes we go through as well. We make sounds, such as hiccuping or coughing noises. We might even laugh so hard that we cry. Our faces change—we use about 15 of our face muscles when we laugh. Our bodies move, twist, or contort. The larynx might half close, making it hard for us to catch our breath or to speak because air can't get into and out of the body as well as it normally can.

Despite the odd things that happen to our bodies as we laugh, scientific studies have shown that laughter can have many positive effects on health. One of those effects is providing a good workout. Laughter works stomach, facial, leg, and back muscles. Studies show that laughing 100 times has the same effect as being on a rowing machine for 10 minutes or an exercise bike for 15 minutes.

HUMAN LAUGHTER		
Physical Health Benefits	**Mental Health Benefits**	**Social Benefits**
Boosts immunity	Adds joy and zest to life	Strengthens relationships
Reduces the effects of stress	Improves memory and learning	Builds confidence
Decreases pain	Relieves stress	Enhances teamwork
Relaxes muscles	Improves mood	Helps defuse conflict
Lowers blood pressure	Enhances resilience	Promotes group bonding

Even if nothing seems funny to you right now, you can create opportunities to laugh in the near future. Try some of these activities, and you'll be laughing in no time:

- Watch a funny movie or TV show.
- Read cartoons or comics.
- Share a good joke or a funny story.
- Check out a book from the humor section at the library.
- Play with a pet.
- Do something silly.
- Plan a fun outing with friends.

Now that you've read about the health benefits of laughter and activities that can make you laugh, you are better prepared to improve your health and the health of those around you with a simple giggle.

UNIT
3

The Benefits of Laughter

Answer Questions

Read and answer each question.

1. Many researchers believe that humans laugh in order to ____.
   - Ⓐ make themselves feel better
   - Ⓑ bond with other humans
   - Ⓒ exercise their stomachs

2. When endorphins are released, a person's ____ is lowered.
   - Ⓐ stress level
   - Ⓑ ability to laugh
   - Ⓒ immune system

3. Which of the following is a social benefit of laughter?
   - Ⓐ enhanced teamwork
   - Ⓑ improved memory
   - Ⓒ fewer infections

4. Laughter is good for your body's overall health because it ____.
   - Ⓐ moves your facial muscles
   - Ⓑ half closes your larynx
   - Ⓒ is a form of physical exercise

5. Why do you think humans enjoy being "part of the group"?

   _____

   _____

6. Describe the last time you laughed really hard. What made you laugh and why?

   _____

   _____

Name _____

Organize Information

Read the health article again. Then write information in the graphic organizer that tells the causes and effects of laughter.

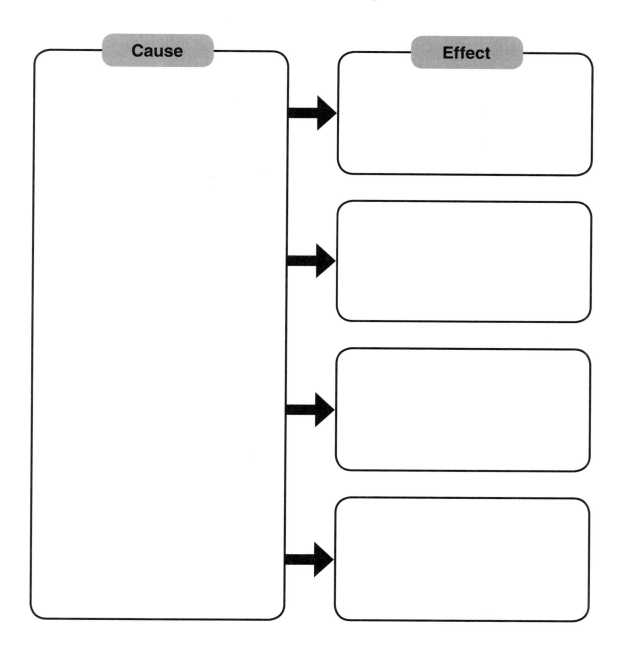

Cause

Effect

Name _____

The Benefits of Laughter

Cause and Effect

Write a cause-and-effect essay about **the benefits of laughter**. Use information from your graphic organizer and the health article.

_____

Title

_____

_____

_____

_____

_____

_____

_____

_____

_____

_____

_____

_____

Name _____

Evaluate Your Writing

Read about the cause-and-effect text structure. Then use your essay to complete the activity below.

> A text that has a **cause-and-effect** structure tells what happens (effect) and why it happens (cause). It also tells if a cause has multiple effects.

The reason for writing is clear.

My essay described the cause-and-effect relationship(s) between: _____

_____

I used these cause-and-effect signal words:

_____   _____   _____

I provided details that support the topic.

I included these detail sentences:

1. _____

2. _____

My paragraphs have a clear focus.

My first paragraph explains that _____

caused (or causes) _____

My last paragraph summarizes the cause-and-effect relationship(s) with this sentence:

_____

Motion Sickness

Lesson Objectives

Writing
Students use information from the health article to write a cause-and-effect essay.

Vocabulary
Students learn content vocabulary words and use those words to write about the cause and effects of motion sickness.

Content Knowledge
Students learn that mixed signals between the body and the brain cause a variety of motion sickness symptoms.

Essential Understanding
Students understand that they can take active steps to prevent or ease motion sickness.

Prepare the Unit

Reproduce and distribute one copy for each student.

1 Unit Focus and Lesson Checklist

Distribute one unit to each student and direct students' attention to the Unit Focus and Lesson Checklist. Tell them they will be able to refer to the focus of the unit as needed while working on the lessons. Instruct students to check off each task on the checklist after they complete it.

Read aloud the focus statements, and verify that students understand their purpose for reading. Ask:

- *What are we going to read about?* (motion sickness)

- *What are you going to learn about it?* (its cause and effects)

- *What are you going to write based on this article?* (a cause-and-effect essay)

 CCSS: **W** 6.1, 6.4, 6.9   **RIT** 6.1, 6.4, 6.10

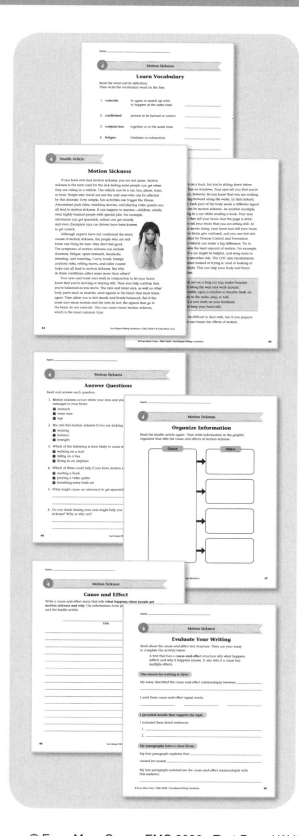

2 Learn Vocabulary

Read aloud each content vocabulary word and have students repeat. Then read aloud and discuss the definitions. Explain that students will have a better understanding of the words after they read the health article. Have students write the vocabulary words on the provided lines.

3 Read the Health Article: *Motion Sickness*

Read aloud the health article as students follow along silently. Then have students reread the article independently or in small groups.

4 Answer Questions About the Health Article

To ensure reading comprehension, have students answer the text-dependent questions. Review the answers together.

5 Organize Information

Explain to students that they will use a cause-and-effect graphic organizer to help them plan their essays. Guide students in using the text to complete the organizer.

6 Write a Cause-and-Effect Essay

Have students complete the writing assignment independently, with a partner, or in small groups.

Review the structure of a cause-and-effect essay and the related signal words:

- Explains what happens (effect) and why it happens (cause)

- Signal words: *because, therefore, so, since, as a result*

7 Evaluate Your Writing

Explain that students will evaluate their writing to ensure that they have produced well-written essays that follow the cause-and-effect text structure.

UNIT 4

Motion Sickness

Unit Focus

You are going to read a health article about motion sickness.

As You Read:

Think about the cause and multiple effects of this illness.

After You Read:

Use information from the article to write a cause-and-effect essay about motion sickness.

Lesson Checklist

Check off each task after you complete it.

- [ ] **Learn Vocabulary**
- [ ] **Read the Health Article:** *Motion Sickness*
- [ ] **Answer Questions About the Health Article**
- [ ] **Organize Information**
- [ ] **Write a Cause-and-Effect Essay**
- [ ] **Evaluate Your Writing**

Name _____

Learn Vocabulary

Read the word and its definition.
Then write the vocabulary word on the line.

1. **coincide**   to agree or match up with;
                       to happen at the same time   _____

2. **confirmed**   proven to be factual or correct   _____

3. **conjunction**   together or at the same time   _____

4. **fatigue**   tiredness or exhaustion   _____

5. **immobile**   being still or not moving   _____

6. **prevention**   the act of stopping an action
                       from happening in advance   _____

7. **static**   motionless   _____

8. **term**   a scientific or technical word
                       that defines a topic or condition   _____

Motion Sickness

If you have ever had motion sickness, you are not alone. Motion sickness is the term used for the sick feeling some people can get when they are riding in a vehicle. The vehicle can be a car, bus, plane, train, or boat. People who travel are not the only ones who can be affected by this disorder. Even simple, fun activities can trigger the illness. Amusement park rides, watching movies, and playing video games can all lead to motion sickness. It can happen to anyone—children, adults, even highly-trained people with special jobs. For example, astronauts can get spacesick, sailors can get seasick, and even champion race car drivers have been known to get carsick.

Although experts have not confirmed the exact causes of motion sickness, the people who are sick know one thing for sure: they *don't* feel good. The symptoms of motion sickness can include dizziness, fatigue, upset stomach, headache, sweating, and vomiting. Curvy roads, bumpy airplane rides, rolling waves, and roller coaster loops can all lead to motion sickness. But why do these conditions affect some more than others?

Your eyes and inner ears work in conjunction to let your brain know that you're moving or staying still. They also help confirm that you're balanced as you move. The eyes and inner ears, as well as other body parts such as muscles, send signals to the brain that most times agree. They allow you to feel steady and firmly balanced. But if the inner ears sense motion and the eyes do not, the signals that go to the brain do not coincide. This can cause visual motion sickness, which is the most common type.

Imagine that you are on a boat, but you're sitting down below the deck in a room that has no windows. Your eyes tell you that you're immobile. Your inner ears, however, let you know that you are rocking back and forth or traveling forward along the water. In that instant, your senses do not agree. Each part of the body sends a different signal to the brain. The result can be motion sickness. As another example, imagine that you're riding in a car while reading a book. Your eyes are looking at a page, so they tell your brain that the page is static. In addition, your muscles tell your brain that you are sitting still. At the same time, as the car moves along, your inner ears tell your brain that you are moving. Your brain gets confused, and you can feel sick.

According to the Centers for Disease Control and Prevention (CDC), where you sit in a vehicle can make a big difference. Try to choose a seat that will have the least amount of motion. For example, sitting in the front seat of a car might be helpful, and wing seats in a plane might give you a smoother ride. The CDC also recommends looking out into the distance instead of trying to read or looking at something within the vehicle. This can help your body and brain take in similar information.

Additional tips include:	• If you are on a long car trip, make frequent stops along the way and walk around. • If possible, open a window to breathe fresh air. • Listen to the radio, sing, or talk. • Place a cool cloth on your forehead. • Try to keep your head still.

Motion sickness can be difficult to deal with, but if you prepare your mind and body, you can lessen the effects of motion.

Name _____

Answer Questions

Read and answer each question.

1. Motion sickness occurs when your eyes and your ___ send conflicting messages to your brain.

    Ⓐ stomach

    Ⓑ inner ears

    Ⓒ legs

2. You can feel motion sickness if you are lacking a sense of ___.

    Ⓐ hearing

    Ⓑ balance

    Ⓒ strength

3. Which of the following is least likely to cause motion sickness?

    Ⓐ walking on a trail

    Ⓑ riding on a bus

    Ⓒ flying in an airplane

4. Which of these could help if you have motion sickness?

    Ⓐ reading a book

    Ⓑ playing a video game

    Ⓒ breathing some fresh air

5. What might cause an astronaut to get spacesick?

    _____

    _____

6. Do you think closing your eyes might help you if you have motion sickness? Why or why not?

    _____

    _____

Name _____

Organize Information

Read the health article again. Then write information in the graphic organizer that tells the cause and effects of motion sickness.

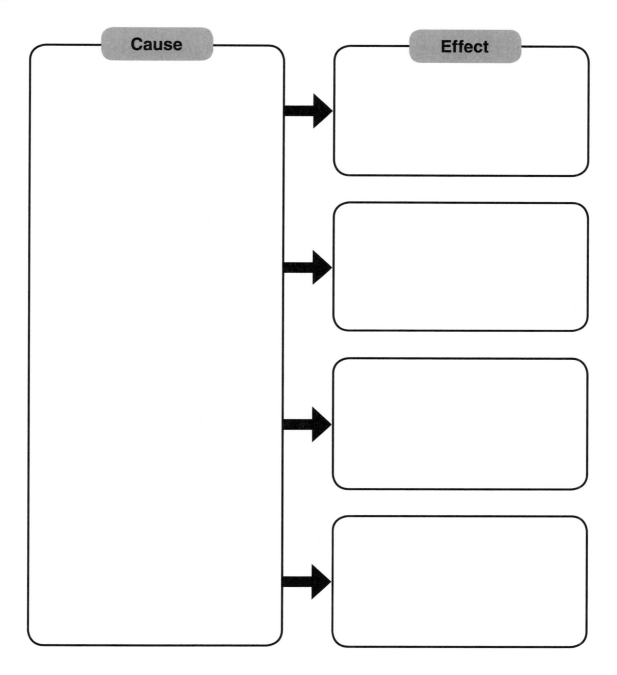

Cause

Effect

Name _____

Cause and Effect

Write a cause-and-effect essay that tells **what happens when people get motion sickness and why.** Use information from your graphic organizer and the health article.

_____

Title

_____

_____

_____

_____

_____

_____

_____

_____

_____

_____

_____

_____

_____

Name _____

Evaluate Your Writing

Read about the cause-and-effect text structure. Then use your essay to complete the activity below.

> A text that has a **cause-and-effect** structure tells what happens (effect) and why it happens (cause). It also tells if a cause has multiple effects.

The reason for writing is clear.

My essay described the cause-and-effect relationship(s) between: _____

_____

I used these cause-and-effect signal words:

_____   _____   _____

I provided details that support the topic.

I included these detail sentences:

1. _____

2. _____

My paragraphs have a clear focus.

My first paragraph explains that _____

caused (or causes) _____

My last paragraph summarizes the cause-and-effect relationship(s) with this sentence:

_____

Jennifer Rodriguez

Lesson Objectives

Writing
Students use information from the biography to write a cause-and-effect essay.

Vocabulary
Students learn content vocabulary words and use those words to write about Jennifer Rodriguez's academic and speed-skating success.

Content Knowledge
Students learn about Jennifer Rodriguez's sporting history, family, and schooling.

Essential Understanding
Students understand that family and schooling can be more rewarding than success in sports.

Prepare the Unit

Reproduce and distribute one copy for each student.

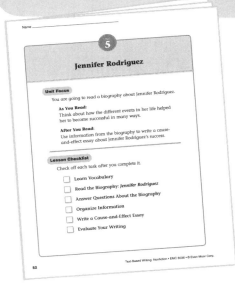

Name _____

5

Jennifer Rodriguez

Unit Focus
You are going to read a biography about Jennifer Rodriguez.

As You Read:
Think about how the different events in her life helped her to become successful in many ways.

After You Read:
Use information from the biography to write a cause-and-effect essay about Jennifer Rodriguez's success.

Lesson Checklist
Check off each task after you complete it.
- [ ] Learn Vocabulary
- [ ] Read the Biography: *Jennifer Rodriguez*
- [ ] Answer Questions About the Biography
- [ ] Organize Information
- [ ] Write a Cause-and-Effect Essay
- [ ] Evaluate Your Writing

Text-Based Writing: Nonfiction • EMC 6036 • © Evan-Moor Corp.

52

1 Unit Focus and Lesson Checklist

Distribute one unit to each student and direct students' attention to the Unit Focus and Lesson Checklist. Tell them they will be able to refer to the focus of the unit as needed while working on the lessons. Instruct students to check off each task on the checklist after they complete it.

Read aloud the focus statements, and verify that students understand their purpose for reading. Ask:

- *Who are we going to read about?* (Jennifer Rodriguez)

- *What are you going to learn about her?* (events in her life and her success)

- *What are you going to write based on this article?* (a cause-and-effect essay)

CCSS: **W** 6.1, 6.4, 6.9   **RIT** 6.1, 6.4, 6.10

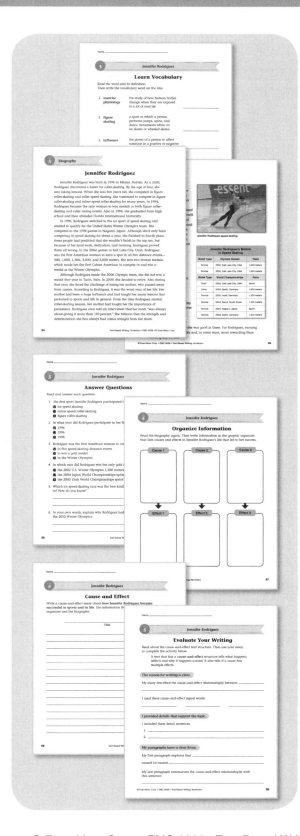

2 Learn Vocabulary

Read aloud each content vocabulary word and have students repeat. Then read aloud and discuss the definitions. Explain that students will have a better understanding of the words after they read the biography. Have students write the vocabulary words on the provided lines.

3 Read the Biography: *Jennifer Rodriguez*

Read aloud the biography as students follow along silently. Then have students reread the biography independently or in small groups.

4 Answer Questions About the Biography

To ensure reading comprehension, have students answer the text-dependent questions. Review the answers together.

5 Organize Information

Explain to students that they will use a cause-and-effect graphic organizer to help them plan their essays. Guide students in using the text to complete the organizer.

6 Write a Cause-and-Effect Essay

Have students complete the writing assignment independently, with a partner, or in small groups.

Review the structure of a cause-and-effect essay and the related signal words:

- Explains what happened (effect) and why it happened (cause)

- Signal words: *because, therefore, so, since, as a result*

7 Evaluate Your Writing

Explain that students will evaluate their writing to ensure that they have produced well-written essays that follow the cause-and-effect text structure.

UNIT
5

Jennifer Rodriguez

Unit Focus

You are going to read a biography about Jennifer Rodriguez.

As You Read:

Think about how the different events in her life helped her to become successful in many ways.

After You Read:

Use information from the biography to write a cause-and-effect essay about Jennifer Rodriguez's success.

Lesson Checklist

Check off each task after you complete it.

- [ ] **Learn Vocabulary**
- [ ] **Read the Biography:** *Jennifer Rodriguez*
- [ ] **Answer Questions About the Biography**
- [ ] **Organize Information**
- [ ] **Write a Cause-and-Effect Essay**
- [ ] **Evaluate Your Writing**

Jennifer Rodriguez

Learn Vocabulary

Read the word and its definition.
Then write the vocabulary word on the line.

1. **exercise physiology**   the study of how human bodies change when they are exposed to a lot of exercise   _____

2. **figure skating**   a sport in which a person performs jumps, spins, and dance movements while on ice skates or wheeled skates   _____

3. **influence**   the power of a person to affect someone in a positive or negative way   _____

4. **persistence**   the act of trying an action over and over again, even if one fails   _____

5. **pertained**   related to; had to do with   _____

6. **qualify**   to be able to participate in an event or on a team as a result of physical training   _____

7. **retire**   to stop working   _____

8. **rigorous**   extremely difficult or demanding   _____

Jennifer Rodriguez

Jennifer Rodriguez was born in 1976 in Miami, Florida. As a child, Rodriguez discovered a talent for roller-skating. By the age of four, she was taking lessons. When she was five years old, she competed in figure roller-skating and roller speed skating. She continued to compete in figure roller-skating and inline speed roller-skating for many years. In 1994, Rodriguez became the only woman to win medals in both figure roller-skating and roller racing events. Also in 1994, she graduated from high school and then attended Florida International University.

In 1996, Rodriguez switched to the ice sport of speed skating and wanted to qualify for the United States Winter Olympics team. She competed in the 1998 games in Nagano, Japan. Although she'd only been competing in speed skating for about a year, she finished in fourth place. Some people had predicted that she wouldn't finish in the top ten, but because of her hard work, dedication, and training, Rodriguez proved them all wrong. In the 2002 games in Salt Lake City, Utah, Rodriguez was the first American woman to earn a spot in all five distance events— 500, 1,000, 1,500, 3,000, and 5,000 meters. She won two bronze medals, which made her the first Cuban American to compete in and win a medal at the Winter Olympics.

Although Rodriguez made the 2006 Olympic team, she did not win a medal that year in Turin, Italy. In 2009, she decided to retire. Also during that year, she faced the challenge of losing her mother, who passed away from cancer. According to Rodriguez, it was the worst year of her life. Her mother had been a huge influence and had taught her many lessons that pertained to sports and life in general. From the time Rodriguez started roller-skating lessons, her mother had taught her the importance of persistence. Rodriguez once told an interviewer that her mom "was always about giving it more than 110 percent." She believes that the strength and determination she has always had comes straight from her mom.

In 2010, Rodriguez decided to return to major competition one last time and compete at the Winter Olympics in Vancouver, Canada. She was determined to have fun and enjoy herself. In the past, Rodriguez had focused only on skating, and the rigorous training took over her entire experience at the games. As an older, mature athlete, she wanted to have balance in 2010. She felt no pressure and, even though she didn't win a medal that year, she had a great time.

In May of 2013, Rodriguez graduated from the University of Miami with a degree in exercise physiology. She was very proud of her academic accomplishment. According to Rodriguez, studying never came as easy to her as skating had. She had participated in sports her whole life—and she *knew* she was good at them. For Rodriguez, earning a college degree was harder and, in some ways, more rewarding than winning any medal.

Jennifer Rodriquez speed skating

Jennifer Rodriguez's Medals in Speed Skating		
Medal Type	**Olympic Games**	**Race**
Bronze	2002; Salt Lake City, Utah	1,000 meters
Bronze	2002; Salt Lake City, Utah	1,500 meters
Medal Type	**World Championships**	**Race**
Gold	2005; Salt Lake City, Utah	Sprint
Silver	2003; Berlin, Germany	1,000 meters
Bronze	2005; Inzell, Germany	1,500 meters
Bronze	2004; Seoul, South Korea	1,500 meters
Bronze	2004; Nagano, Japan	Sprint
Bronze	2003; Berlin, Germany	1,500 meters

Jennifer Rodriguez

Answer Questions

Read and answer each question.

1. The first sport Jennifer Rodriguez participated in was ____.
   - Ⓐ ice speed skating
   - Ⓑ inline speed roller-skating
   - Ⓒ figure roller-skating

2. In what year did Rodriguez participate in her first Winter Olympics?
   - Ⓐ 1994
   - Ⓑ 1996
   - Ⓒ 1998

3. Rodriguez was the first American woman to compete ____.
   - Ⓐ in five speed-skating distance events
   - Ⓑ to win a gold medal
   - Ⓒ in the Winter Olympics

4. In which race did Rodriguez win her only gold medal?
   - Ⓐ the 2002 U.S. Winter Olympics 1,500 meters
   - Ⓑ the 2004 Japan World Championships sprint
   - Ⓒ the 2005 Utah World Championships sprint

5. Which ice speed-skating race was the best kind for Rodriguez to compete in? How do you know?

   _____

   _____

6. In your own words, explain why Rodriguez had such a nice time at the 2010 Winter Olympics.

   _____

   _____

UNIT
5

Jennifer Rodriguez

Organize Information

Read the biography again. Then write information in the graphic organizer that lists causes and effects in Jennifer Rodriguez's life that led to her success.

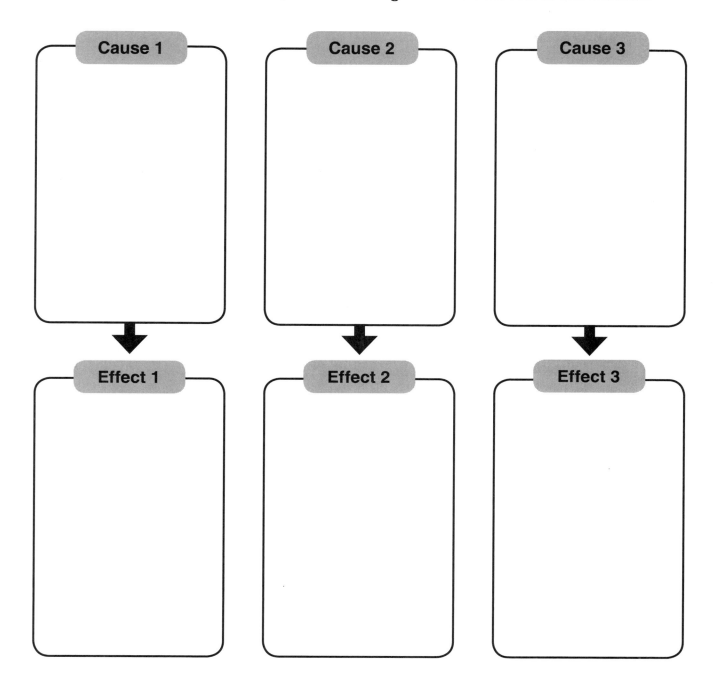

Cause 1

Cause 2

Cause 3

Effect 1

Effect 2

Effect 3

Name _____

Cause and Effect

Write a cause-and-effect essay about **how Jennifer Rodriguez became successful in sports and in life**. Use information from your graphic organizer and the biography.

_____
Title

_____

_____

_____

_____

_____

_____

_____

_____

_____

_____

_____

_____

_____

_____

UNIT
5

Evaluate Your Writing

Read about the cause-and-effect text structure. Then use your essay to complete the activity below.

> A text that has a **cause-and-effect** structure tells what happens (effect) and why it happens (cause). It also tells if a cause has multiple effects.

The reason for writing is clear.

My essay described the cause-and-effect relationship(s) between: _____

_____

I used these cause-and-effect signal words:

_____   _____   _____

I provided details that support the topic.

I included these detail sentences:

1. _____

2. _____

My paragraphs have a clear focus.

My first paragraph explains that _____

caused (or causes) _____

My last paragraph summarizes the cause-and-effect relationship(s) with this sentence:

_____

Fancy Fliers

Lesson Objectives

Writing
Students use information from the science article to write an explanatory essay.

Vocabulary
Students learn content vocabulary words and use those words to write about how hummingbirds work to survive.

Content Knowledge
Students learn about the habitats, food sources, and adaptations of hummingbirds.

Essential Understanding
Students understand that certain plants and animals work together and rely on each other to survive.

Prepare the Unit

Reproduce and distribute one copy for each student.

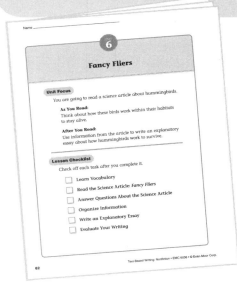

1 Unit Focus and Lesson Checklist

Distribute one unit to each student and direct students' attention to the Unit Focus and Lesson Checklist. Tell them they will be able to refer to the focus of the unit as needed while working on the lessons. Instruct students to check off each task on the checklist after they complete it.

Read aloud the focus statements, and verify that students understand their purpose for reading. Ask:

- *What are we going to read about?* (hummingbirds)

- *What are you going to learn about them?* (how they work to stay alive)

- *What are you going to write based on this article?* (an explanatory essay)

CCSS: **W** 6.1, 6.4, 6.9   **RIT** 6.1, 6.4, 6.10

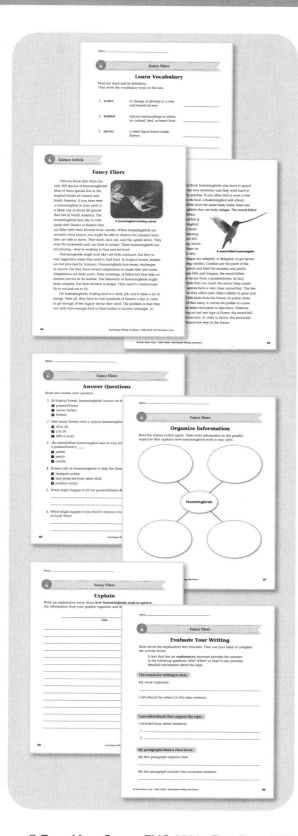

2 Learn Vocabulary

Read aloud each content vocabulary word and have students repeat. Then read aloud and discuss the definitions. Explain that students will have a better understanding of the words after they read the science article. Have students write the vocabulary words on the provided lines.

3 Read the Science Article: *Fancy Fliers*

Read aloud the science article as students follow along silently. Then have students reread the article independently or in small groups.

4 Answer Questions About the Science Article

To ensure reading comprehension, have students answer the text-dependent questions. Review the answers together.

5 Organize Information

Explain to students that they will use an idea-web graphic organizer to help them plan their essays. Guide students in using the text to complete the organizer.

6 Write an Explanatory Essay

Have students complete the writing assignment independently, with a partner, or in small groups.

Review the structure of an explanatory essay:

- Provides the answers to the following questions: *Why? Where?* or *How?*

- Includes detailed information about the topic

- Includes an introductory topic sentence and a conclusion sentence at the end

7 Evaluate Your Writing

Explain that students will evaluate their writing to ensure that they have produced well-written essays that follow the explanatory text structure.

UNIT 6

Fancy Fliers

Unit Focus

You are going to read a science article about hummingbirds.

As You Read:

Think about how these birds work within their habitats to stay alive.

After You Read:

Use information from the article to write an explanatory essay about how hummingbirds work to survive.

Lesson Checklist

Check off each task after you complete it.

☐ **Learn Vocabulary**

☐ **Read the Science Article:** *Fancy Fliers*

☐ **Answer Questions About the Science Article**

☐ **Organize Information**

☐ **Write an Explanatory Essay**

☐ **Evaluate Your Writing**

Fancy Fliers

Learn Vocabulary

Read the word and its definition.
Then write the vocabulary word on the line.

1. **evolve**   to change or develop in a new
                     and beneficial way   _____

2. **habitat**   natural surroundings in which
                     an animal, bird, or insect lives   _____

3. **nectar**   a sweet liquid found inside
                     flowers   _____

4. **observe**   to watch or study carefully   _____

5. **pistils**   the female reproductive parts
                     of flowers (the seeds develop
                     here)   _____

6. **stamens**   the male reproductive parts
                     of flowers (the pollen is
                     produced here)   _____

7. **territorial**   defensive or protective of one's
                     space or area   _____

8. **traits**   characteristics   _____

Fancy Fliers

Did you know that there are over 300 species of hummingbirds? Most of these species live in the tropical forests of Central and South America. If you have seen a hummingbird in your yard, it is likely one of about 20 species that live in North America. The hummingbirds here like to visit yards with flowers or feeders that

A hummingbird drinking nectar

are filled with their favorite food—nectar. When hummingbirds are around a food source, you might be able to observe the unusual ways they are able to move. They dash, dart, zip, and flip upside down. They even fly backwards and can float in midair. These hummingbirds are not playing—they're working to find and eat food.

Hummingbirds might look like cute little creatures, but they're very aggressive when they need to find food. In tropical forests, feeders are not provided by humans. Hummingbirds face many challenges in nature, but they have several adaptations to make their job easier. Adaptations are body parts, body coverings, or behaviors that help an animal survive in its habitat. The behaviors of hummingbirds might seem complex, but their mission is simple. They need to continuously fly to eat and eat to fly.

For hummingbirds, finding food is a daily job, and it takes a lot of energy. After all, they have to visit hundreds of flowers a day in order to get enough of the sugary nectar they need. The problem is that they can only store enough food in their bodies to survive overnight. In addition to having to find food, hummingbirds also have to guard their food sources. They are very territorial and they work hard to guard their favorite flower patches. If any other bird or even a bee or a butterfly tries to take its food, a hummingbird will attack.

While all hummingbirds have the same basic traits, there are some species of hummingbirds that are truly unique. The sword-billed hummingbird of South Africa is one example. The sword-bill is one of the largest hummingbird species, not because of its body size but because of the amazing length of its bill. This bird's bill can be up to 4 inches long, which is about 3 inches longer than its body! The bird's tongue is also

A sword-billed hummingbird

very long. The bill and tongue are adapted, or designed, to get nectar from flowers that have long corollas. Corollas are the parts of the flowers that include the petals and hold the stamens and pistils.

Because of their unique bills and tongues, the sword-billed hummingbirds can drink nectar from a passionflower. In fact, sword-bills are the only birds that can reach the nectar deep inside these flowers. These two species have a very close connection. The two of them evolve together, so they affect each other's ability to grow and survive. When the sword-bill feeds from the flower, its pollen sticks to the bird. When the bird flies away, it carries the pollen to a new passionflower, which then helps that plant to reproduce. However, experts say that by feeding on just one type of flower, the sword-bill could become at risk of extinction. In order to thrive, the sword-bill may need to adapt in a brand-new way in the future.

Fancy Fliers

Answer Questions

Read and answer each question.

1. In tropical forests, hummingbirds cannot eat from ____.
   - Ⓐ passionflowers
   - Ⓑ nectar feeders
   - Ⓒ flowers

2. How many flowers does a typical hummingbird need to visit each day?
   - Ⓐ 10 to 20
   - Ⓑ 2 to 50
   - Ⓒ 200 or more

3. The sword-billed hummingbird uses its long bill to get nectar from a passionflower's ____.
   - Ⓐ pollen
   - Ⓑ petals
   - Ⓒ corolla

4. Flowers rely on hummingbirds to help the flowers ____.
   - Ⓐ transport pollen
   - Ⓑ stay protected from other birds
   - Ⓒ produce nectar

5. What might happen if all the passionflowers died off?

   _____

   _____

6. What might happen if you tried to remove a hummingbird's sources of food? Why?

   _____

   _____

Organize Information

Read the science article again. Then write information in the graphic organizer that explains how hummingbirds work to stay alive.

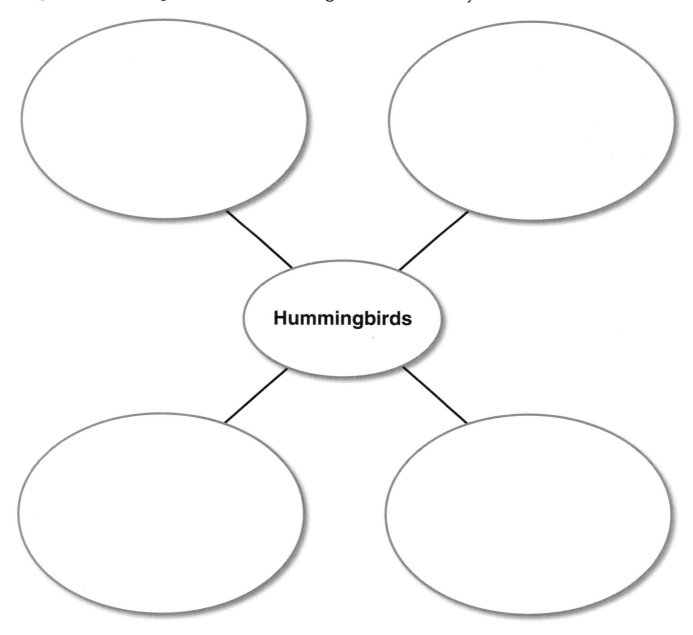

Hummingbirds

UNIT
6

Explain

Write an explanatory essay about **how hummingbirds work to survive**.
Use information from your graphic organizer and the science article.

_____
Title

_____

_____

_____

_____

_____

_____

_____

_____

_____

_____

_____

_____

_____

_____

_____

Name _____

UNIT 6

Evaluate Your Writing

Read about the explanatory text structure. Then use your essay to complete the activity below.

A text that has an **explanatory** structure provides the answers to the following questions: *Why? Where?* or *How?* It also provides detailed information about the topic.

The reason for writing is clear.

My essay explained:

_____

I introduced the subject in this topic sentence:

_____

I provided details that support the topic.

I included these detail sentences:

   1. _____

   2. _____

My paragraphs have a clear focus.

My first paragraph explains that:

_____

My last paragraph includes this conclusion sentence:

_____

The United Nations

Lesson Objectives

Writing
Students use information from the social studies article to write an explanatory essay.

Vocabulary
Students learn content vocabulary words and use those words to write about why the United Nations is so important to the world.

Content Knowledge
Students learn why the United Nations was formed and how it functions today.

Essential Understanding
Students understand that the United Nations is beneficial to the entire world because of its donations and work for worldwide peace.

Prepare the Unit

Reproduce and distribute one copy for each student.

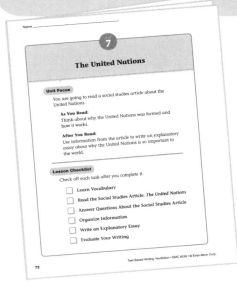

1 Unit Focus and Lesson Checklist

Distribute one unit to each student and direct students' attention to the Unit Focus and Lesson Checklist. Tell them they will be able to refer to the focus of the unit as needed while working on the lessons. Instruct students to check off each task on the checklist after they complete it.

Read aloud the focus statements, and verify that students understand their purpose for reading. Ask:

- *What are we going to read about?* (the United Nations)

- *What are you going to learn about it?* (why it was formed and how it works)

- *What are you going to write based on this article?* (an explanatory essay)

CCSS: **W** 6.1, 6.4, 6.9 **RIT** 6.1, 6.4, 6.10

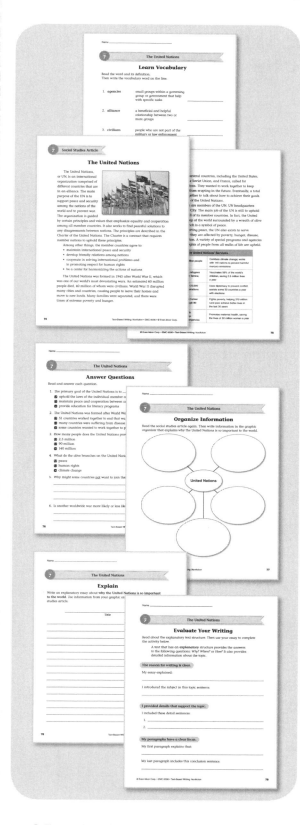

2. Learn Vocabulary

Read aloud each content vocabulary word and have students repeat. Then read aloud and discuss the definitions. Explain that students will have a better understanding of the words after they read the social studies article. Have students write the vocabulary words on the provided lines.

3. Read the Social Studies Article: *The United Nations*

Read aloud the social studies article as students follow along silently. Then have students reread the article independently or in small groups.

4. Answer Questions About the Social Studies Article

To ensure reading comprehension, have students answer the text-dependent questions. Review the answers together.

5. Organize Information

Explain to students that they will use an idea-web graphic organizer to help them plan their essays. Guide students in using the text to complete the organizer.

6. Write an Explanatory Essay

Have students complete the writing assignment independently, with a partner, or in small groups.

Review the structure of an explanatory essay:

- Provides the answers to the following questions: *Why? Where?* or *How?*

- Includes detailed information about the topic

- Includes an introductory topic sentence and a conclusion sentence at the end

7. Evaluate Your Writing

Explain that students will evaluate their writing to ensure that they have produced well-written essays that follow the explanatory text structure.

UNIT
7

The United Nations

Unit Focus

You are going to read a social studies article about the United Nations.

As You Read:

Think about why the United Nations was formed and how it works.

After You Read:

Use information from the article to write an explanatory essay about why the United Nations is so important to the world.

Lesson Checklist

Check off each task after you complete it.

☐ Learn Vocabulary

☐ Read the Social Studies Article: *The United Nations*

☐ Answer Questions About the Social Studies Article

☐ Organize Information

☐ Write an Explanatory Essay

☐ Evaluate Your Writing

Name _____

Learn Vocabulary

Read the word and its definition.
Then write the vocabulary word on the line.

1. **agencies**   small groups within a governing group or government that help with specific tasks   _____

2. **alliance**   a beneficial and helpful relationship between two or more groups   _____

3. **civilians**   people who are not part of the military or law enforcement   _____

4. **contract**   a written agreement signed by two or more parties   _____

5. **human rights**   the basic freedoms that every person deserves   _____

6. **illiteracy**   the inability to read or write   _____

7. **principles**   rules or laws   _____

8. **values**   ideas that people believe in or feel are very important   _____

The United Nations

The United Nations, or UN, is an international organization comprised of different countries that are in an alliance. The main purpose of the UN is to support peace and security among the nations of the world and to prevent war. The organization is guided

by certain principles and values that emphasize equality and cooperation among all member countries. It also works to find peaceful solutions to any disagreements between nations. The principles are described in the Charter of the United Nations. The Charter is a contract that requires member nations to uphold these principles.

Among other things, the member countries agree to:

- maintain international peace and security
- develop friendly relations among nations
- cooperate in solving international problems and in promoting respect for human rights
- be a center for harmonizing the actions of nations

The United Nations was formed in 1945 after World War II, which was one of our world's most devastating wars. An estimated 60 million people died, 40 million of whom were civilians. World War II disrupted many cities and countries, causing people to leave their homes and move to new lands. Many families were separated, and there were times of extreme poverty and hunger.

After World War II, several countries, including the United States, China, Great Britain, the Soviet Union, and France, called for cooperation among nations. They wanted to work together to keep another worldwide war from erupting in the future. Eventually, a total of 51 countries came together to talk about how to achieve their goals. That was the beginning of the United Nations.

Today, 193 countries are members of the UN. UN headquarters are located in New York City. The main job of the UN is still to uphold peace and security for all of its member countries. In fact, the United Nations' emblem is a map of the world surrounded by a wreath of olive branches. The olive branch is a symbol of peace.

In addition to supporting peace, the UN also exists to serve people in need, whether they are affected by poverty, hunger, disease, illiteracy, or discrimination. A variety of special programs and agencies exist to make sure the rights of people from all walks of life are upheld.

The United Nations' Services	
Provides food to 90 million people in 75 countries	Combats climate change; works with 140 nations to prevent harmful mercury emissions
Assists over 34 million refugees and people fleeing war, famine, or persecution	Vaccinates 58% of the world's children, saving 2.5 million lives a year
Keeps the peace with 120,000 peacekeepers in 16 operations on 4 continents	Uses diplomacy to prevent conflict; assists some 50 countries a year with elections
Protects and promotes human rights on-site and through 80 treaties/declarations	Fights poverty, helping 370 million rural poor achieve better lives in the last 30 years
Mobilizes $12.5 billion in humanitarian aid to help people affected by emergencies	Promotes maternal health, saving the lives of 30 million women a year

The United Nations

Answer Questions

Read and answer each question.

1. The primary goal of the United Nations is to ____.
   - Ⓐ uphold the laws of the individual member countries
   - Ⓑ maintain peace and cooperation between countries
   - Ⓒ provide education for literacy programs

2. The United Nations was formed after World War II because ____.
   - Ⓐ 51 countries worked together to end that war
   - Ⓑ many countries were suffering from disease and discrimination
   - Ⓒ some countries wanted to work together to prevent future wars

3. How many people does the United Nations provide food for?
   - Ⓐ 2.5 million
   - Ⓑ 90 million
   - Ⓒ 140 million

4. What do the olive branches on the United Nations' emblem symbolize?
   - Ⓐ peace
   - Ⓑ human rights
   - Ⓒ climate change

5. Why might some countries not want to join the United Nations?

   _____

   _____

   _____

6. Is another worldwide war more likely or less likely to happen today? Why?

   _____

   _____

Organize Information

Read the social studies article again. Then write information in the graphic organizer that explains why the United Nations is so important to the world.

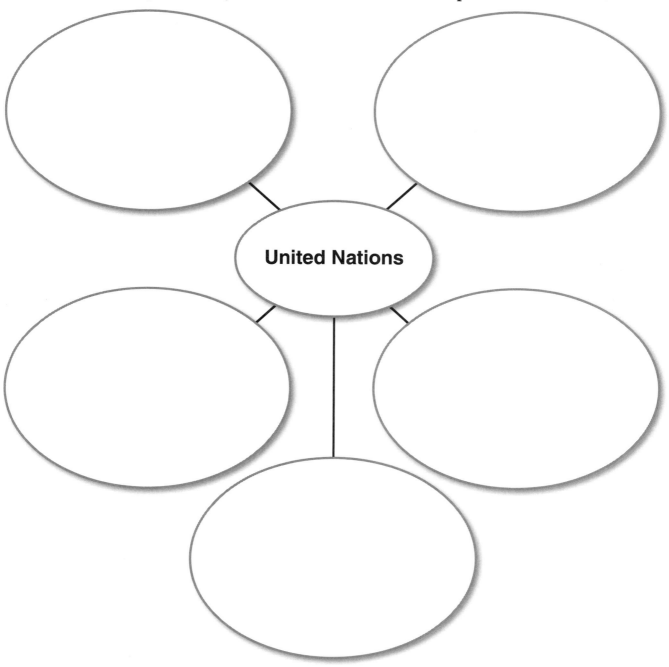

United Nations

Name _____

The United Nations

Explain

Write an explanatory essay about **why the United Nations is so important to the world**. Use information from your graphic organizer and the social studies article.

_____

Title

_____

_____

_____

_____

_____

_____

_____

_____

_____

_____

_____

_____

UNIT 7

The United Nations

Evaluate Your Writing

Read about the explanatory text structure. Then use your essay to complete the activity below.

> A text that has an **explanatory** structure provides the answers to the following questions: *Why? Where?* or *How?* It also provides detailed information about the topic.

The reason for writing is clear.

My essay explained:

_____

I introduced the subject in this topic sentence:

_____

I provided details that support the topic.

I included these detail sentences:

1. _____

2. _____

My paragraphs have a clear focus.

My first paragraph explains that:

_____

My last paragraph includes this conclusion sentence:

_____

Koa Halpern

Lesson Objectives

Writing
Students use information from the biography to write an opinion essay.

Vocabulary
Students learn content vocabulary words and use those words to write about whether Koa Halpern will or will not make a difference in the world.

Content Knowledge
Students learn about fastfoodfree.org and how Koa Halpern is working to help others.

Essential Understanding
Students understand that because Koa Halpern started helping others at such a young age, he will most likely continue to do so in the future.

Prepare the Unit

Reproduce and distribute one copy for each student.

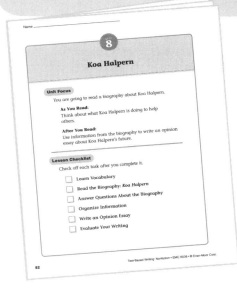

1 Unit Focus and Lesson Checklist

Distribute one unit to each student and direct students' attention to the Unit Focus and Lesson Checklist. Tell them they will be able to refer to the focus of the unit as needed while working on the lessons. Instruct students to check off each task on the checklist after they complete it.

Read aloud the focus statements, and verify that students understand their purpose for reading. Ask:

• *Who are we going to read about?* (Koa Halpern)

• *What are you going to learn about him?* (what he is doing to help others)

• *What are you going to write based on this biography?* (an opinion essay)

CCSS: 6.2, 6.4, 6.9   6.1, 6.4, 6.10

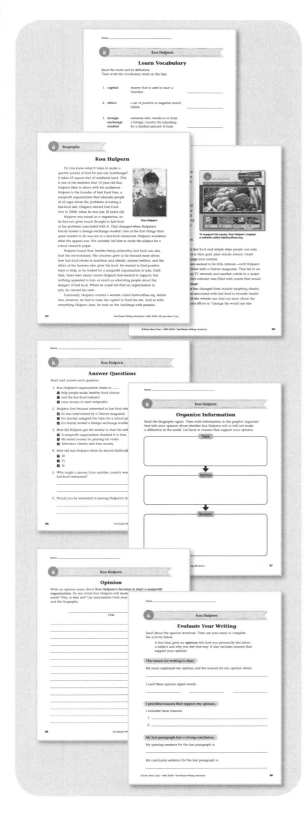

2 Learn Vocabulary

Read aloud each content vocabulary word and have students repeat. Then read aloud and discuss the definitions. Explain that students will have a better understanding of the words after they read the biography. Have students write the vocabulary words on the provided lines.

3 Read the Biography: *Koa Halpern*

Read aloud the biography as students follow along silently. Then have students reread the biography independently or in small groups.

4 Answer Questions About the Biography

To ensure reading comprehension, have students answer the text-dependent questions. Review the answers together.

5 Organize Information

Explain to students that they will use an opinion graphic organizer to help them plan their essays. Guide students in using the text to complete the organizer.

6 Write an Opinion Essay

Have students complete the writing assignment independently, with a partner, or in small groups.

Remind students that an opinion essay:

- tells how you feel about something,
- tells why you feel that way, and
- includes signal words: *I feel, I think, to me, I like, I agree that; I don't like, I disagree that.*

7 Evaluate Your Writing

Explain that students will evaluate their writing to ensure that they have produced well-written essays that follow the opinion structure.

UNIT 8

Koa Halpern

Unit Focus

You are going to read a biography about Koa Halpern.

As You Read:

Think about what Koa Halpern is doing to help others.

After You Read:

Use information from the biography to write an opinion essay about Koa Halpern's future.

Lesson Checklist

Check off each task after you complete it.

- [ ] **Learn Vocabulary**
- [ ] **Read the Biography:** *Koa Halpern*
- [ ] **Answer Questions About the Biography**
- [ ] **Organize Information**
- [ ] **Write an Opinion Essay**
- [ ] **Evaluate Your Writing**

Koa Halpern

Learn Vocabulary

Read the word and its definition.
Then write the vocabulary word on the line.

1. **capital** — money that is used to start a business _____

2. **ethics** — a set of positive or negative moral beliefs _____

3. **foreign exchange student** — someone who travels to or from a foreign country for schooling for a limited amount of time _____

4. **nonprofit** — an organization that does work as a public service, not to earn money _____

5. **obesity** — the state of being overweight _____

6. **vegetarian** — a person who does not eat meat, and sometimes no animal products _____

7. **welfare** — the state of being healthy or doing well; well-being _____

Koa Halpern

Do you know what it takes to make a quarter pound of beef for just one hamburger? It takes 55 square feet of rainforest land. This is one of the statistics that 15-year-old Koa Halpern likes to share with his audiences. Halpern is the founder of Fast Food Free, a nonprofit organization that educates people of all ages about the problems of eating a fast-food diet. Halpern started Fast Food Free in 2008, when he was just 10 years old.

Koa Halpern

Halpern was raised as a vegetarian, so he had not given much thought to fast food or the problems associated with it. That changed when Halpern's family hosted a foreign exchange student. One of the first things their guest wanted to do was eat at a fast-food restaurant. Halpern wondered what the appeal was. His curiosity led him to study the subject for a school research paper.

Halpern found that, besides being unhealthy, fast food can also hurt the environment. His concerns grew as he learned more about how fast food relates to nutrition and obesity, animal welfare, and the ethics of the farmers who grow the food. He wanted to find positive ways to help, so he looked for a nonprofit organization to join. Until then, there were many causes Halpern had wanted to support, but nothing appealed to him as much as educating people about the dangers of fast food. When he could not find an organization to join, he created his own.

Eventually, Halpern created a website called fastfoodfree.org. Before that, however, he had to raise the capital to fund the site. And as with everything Halpern does, he took on the challenge with passion.

Koa Halpern, continued

Halpern played his violin at the 16th Street Mall in his hometown of Denver, Colorado, to earn the money he needed. Now it was time for the real work.

The goal of Fast Food Free was to "get people to eat less fast food through education and community awareness, which results in healthier people and a better world." On his website, Halpern provides information about the

To support his cause, Koa Halpern created a website called fastfoodfree.org.

problems associated with fast food and simple steps people can take to change their habits: set a clear goal, plan snacks ahead, create a buddy system, and change your routine.

In the beginning, there seemed to be little interest—until Halpern got a request for an interview with a Denver magazine. That led to an appearance on a national TV network and another article in a major newspaper. Soon, Halpern's calendar was filled with events that would help him spread his message.

Today, Fast Food Free has changed from mainly targeting obesity and environmental issues associated with fast food to broader health concerns. People who visit the website can find out more about the organization and Halpern's efforts to "change the world one bite at a time."

Name _____

Answer Questions

Read and answer each question.

1. Koa Halpern's organization works to ____.
   - Ⓐ help people make healthy food choices
   - Ⓑ end the fast-food industry
   - Ⓒ raise money to start nonprofits

2. Halpern first became interested in fast food when ____.
   - Ⓐ he was interviewed by a Denver magazine
   - Ⓑ his teacher assigned the topic for a school project
   - Ⓒ his family hosted a foreign exchange student

3. How did Halpern get the money to start his website?
   - Ⓐ A nonprofit organization donated it to him.
   - Ⓑ He raised money by playing his violin.
   - Ⓒ Television viewers sent him money.

4. How old was Halpern when he started fastfoodfree.org?
   - Ⓐ 10
   - Ⓑ 15
   - Ⓒ 16

5. Why might a person from another country want to visit an American fast-food restaurant?

   _____

   _____

6. Would you be interested in joining Halpern's organization? Why or why not?

   _____

   _____

Name _____

Organize Information

Read the biography again. Then write information in the graphic organizer that tells your opinion about whether Koa Halpern will or will not make a difference in the world. List facts or reasons that support your opinion.

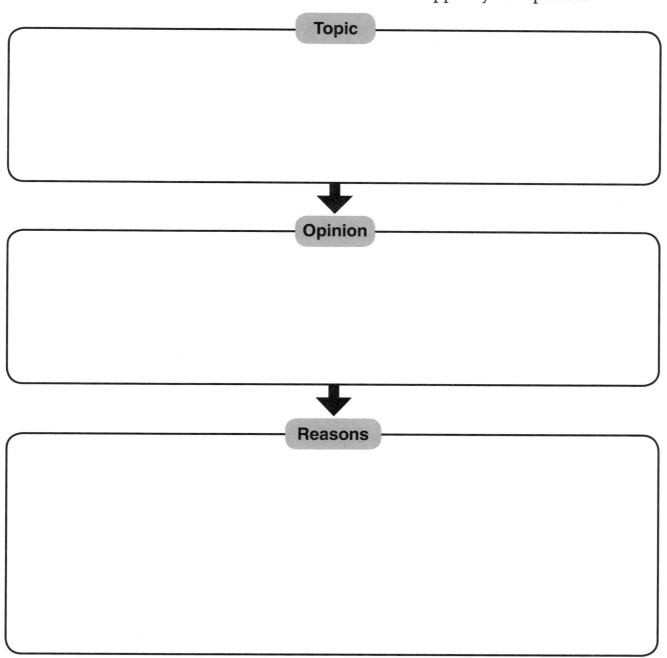

Topic

Opinion

Reasons

Opinion

Write an opinion essay about **Koa Halpern's decision to start a nonprofit organization**. Do you think Koa Halpern will make a difference in the world? Why or why not? Use information from your graphic organizer and the biography.

_____

Title

_____

_____

_____

_____

_____

_____

_____

_____

_____

_____

_____

_____

Name _____

Koa Halpern

Evaluate Your Writing

Read about the opinion structure. Then use your essay to complete the activity below.

A text that gives an **opinion** tells how you personally feel about a subject and why you feel that way. It also includes reasons that support your opinion.

The reason for writing is clear.

My essay explained my opinion and the reasons for my opinion about:

_____

I used these opinion signal words:

_____   _____   _____

I provided reasons that support my opinion.

I included these reasons:

1. _____

2. _____

My last paragraph has a strong conclusion.

My opening sentence for the last paragraph is:

_____

My conclusion sentence for the last paragraph is:

_____

Safety First

Lesson Objectives

Writing
Students use information from the social studies article to write an opinion essay.

Vocabulary
Students learn content vocabulary words and use those words to write about whether they do or do not need to be prepared for any kind of emergency or disaster.

Content Knowledge
Students learn about the types of disasters and why they should be prepared for them.

Essential Understanding
Students understand that knowing their specific geographical and weather-related risks can help them be prepared and save lives.

Prepare the Unit

Reproduce and distribute one copy for each student.

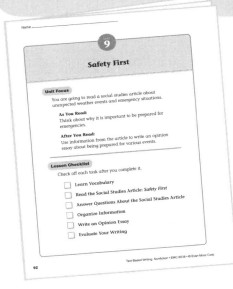

1 Unit Focus and Lesson Checklist

Distribute one unit to each student and direct students' attention to the Unit Focus and Lesson Checklist. Tell them they will be able to refer to the focus of the unit as needed while working on the lessons. Instruct students to check off each task on the checklist after they complete it.

Read aloud the focus statements, and verify that students understand their purpose for reading. Ask:

- *What are we going to read about?* (unexpected weather events)

- *What are you going to learn about them?* (why it is important to be prepared for emergencies)

- *What are you going to write based on this article?* (an opinion essay)

CCSS: **W** 6.2, 6.4, 6.9   **RIT** 6.1, 6.4, 6.10

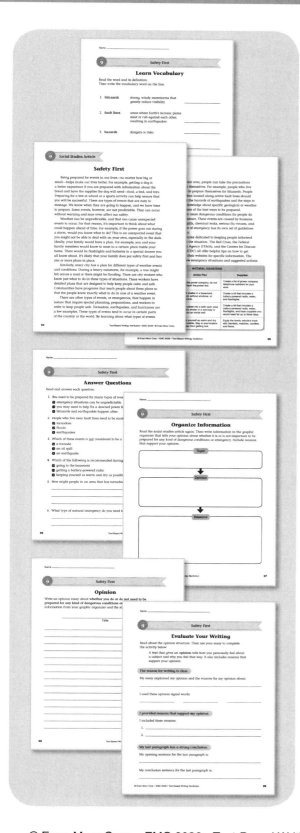

2 Learn Vocabulary

Read aloud each content vocabulary word and have students repeat. Then read aloud and discuss the definitions. Explain that students will have a better understanding of the words after they read the social studies article. Have students write the vocabulary words on the provided lines.

3 Read the Social Studies Article: *Safety First*

Read aloud the social studies article as students follow along silently. Then have students reread the article independently or in small groups.

4 Answer Questions About the Social Studies Article

To ensure reading comprehension, have students answer the text-dependent questions. Review the answers together.

5 Organize Information

Explain to students that they will use an opinion graphic organizer to help them plan their essays. Guide students in using the text to complete the organizer.

6 Write an Opinion Essay

Have students complete the writing assignment independently, with a partner, or in small groups.

Remind students that an opinion essay:

- tells how you feel about something,

- tells why you feel that way, and

- includes signal words: *I feel, I think, to me, I like, I agree that; I don't like, I disagree that.*

7 Evaluate Your Writing

Explain that students will evaluate their writing to ensure that they have produced well-written essays that follow the opinion structure.

UNIT 9

Safety First

Unit Focus

You are going to read a social studies article about unexpected weather events and emergency situations.

As You Read:

Think about why it is important to be prepared for emergencies.

After You Read:

Use information from the article to write an opinion essay about being prepared for various events.

Lesson Checklist

Check off each task after you complete it.

- [ ] **Learn Vocabulary**
- [ ] **Read the Social Studies Article:** *Safety First*
- [ ] **Answer Questions About the Social Studies Article**
- [ ] **Organize Information**
- [ ] **Write an Opinion Essay**
- [ ] **Evaluate Your Writing**

Learn Vocabulary

Read the word and its definition.
Then write the vocabulary word on the line.

1. **blizzards**   strong, windy snowstorms that greatly reduce visibility   _____

2. **fault lines**   areas where Earth's tectonic plates meet or rub against each other, resulting in earthquakes   _____

3. **hazards**   dangers or risks   _____

4. **hurricanes**   large, dangerous storms that begin over the ocean   _____

5. **manage**   to take care of and make decisions about   _____

6. **precautions**   positive actions taken in advance of an event or emergency; preparations   _____

7. **predictable**   expected   _____

8. **tornadoes**   strong, swirling windstorms that happen on land   _____

Safety First

Being prepared for events in our lives—no matter how big or small—helps make our lives better. For example, getting a dog is a better experience if you are prepared with information about the breed and have the supplies the dog will need—food, a bed, and toys. Preparing for a test at school or a sports activity can help ensure that you will be successful. These are types of events that are easy to manage. We know when they are going to happen, and we have time to prepare. Some events, however, are not predictable. They can occur without warning and may even affect our safety.

Weather can be unpredictable, and that can cause unexpected events to occur. For that reason, it's important to think about what could happen ahead of time. For example, if the power goes out during a storm, would you know what to do? This is an unexpected event that you might not be able to deal with on your own, especially in the dark. Ideally, your family would have a plan. For example, you and your family members would know to meet in a certain place inside your home. There would be flashlights and batteries in a special drawer you all know about. It's likely that your family does put safety first and has one or more plans in place.

Similarly, every city has a plan for different types of weather events and conditions. During a heavy rainstorm, for example, a tree might fall across a road or there might be flooding. There are city workers who know just what to do in these types of situations. These workers have detailed plans that are designed to help keep people calm and safe. Communities have programs that teach people about these plans so that the people know exactly what to do in case of a weather event.

There are other types of events, or emergencies, that happen in nature that require special planning, preparations, and workers in order to keep people safe. Tornadoes, earthquakes, and hurricanes are a few examples. These types of events tend to occur in certain parts of the country or the world. By learning about what types of events

Text-Based Writing: Nonfiction • EMC 6036 • © Evan-Moor Corp.

can happen in a particular area, people can take the precautions necessary to help protect themselves. For example, people who live where it snows are likely to prepare themselves for blizzards. People who live in cities and towns located along active fault lines should know all they can about the hazards of earthquakes and the steps to take when one occurs. Knowledge about specific geological or weather hazards in your area is one of the best ways to be prepared.

Some events that can cause dangerous conditions for people do not occur as a result of nature. These events are caused by humans. Some examples are oil spills, chemical leaks, serious flu viruses, and some wildfires. Each type of emergency has its own set of guidelines for response and recovery.

There are many agencies dedicated to keeping people informed and safe no matter what the situation. The Red Cross, the Federal Emergency Management Agency (FEMA), and the Centers for Disease Control and Prevention (CDC) all offer helpful tips on how to get prepared. You can go to their websites for specific information. The chart below lists just a few emergency situations and suggested actions.

NATURAL DISASTERS		
Emergency Situation	**Action Plan**	**Supplies**
Downed Power Line	Call the power company; do not approach the power line.	Create a list of power company telephone numbers for your area.
Tornado	Seek shelter in a basement, a room without windows, or a bathtub.	Create a kit that includes a battery-powered radio, water, and flashlights.
Earthquake	Go outside into a safe open area or take shelter in a doorway or against an inside wall.	Create a kit that includes a battery-powered radio, water, flashlights, and basic supplies you would need for up to three days.
Blizzard	Keep yourself as warm and dry as possible. Stay in one location to keep from getting lost.	Equip the family vehicle's trunk with blankets, matches, candles, and flares.

Safety First

Answer Questions

Read and answer each question.

1. You need to be prepared for many types of events because ____.
   Ⓐ emergency situations can be unpredictable
   Ⓑ you may need to help fix a downed power line
   Ⓒ blizzards and earthquakes happen often

2. People who live near fault lines need to be most prepared for ____.
   Ⓐ tornadoes
   Ⓑ floods
   Ⓒ earthquakes

3. Which of these events is <u>not</u> considered to be a result of nature?
   Ⓐ a tornado
   Ⓑ an oil spill
   Ⓒ an earthquake

4. Which of the following is recommended during a blizzard?
   Ⓐ going to the basement
   Ⓑ getting a battery-powered radio
   Ⓒ keeping yourself as warm and dry as possible

5. How might people in an area that has tornadoes prepare for a disaster?

   _____

   _____

   _____

6. What type of natural emergency do you need to be most prepared for? Why?

   _____

   _____

Name _____

Organize Information

Read the social studies article again. Then write information in the graphic organizer that tells your opinion about whether it is or is not important to be prepared for any kind of dangerous conditions or emergency. Include reasons that support your opinion.

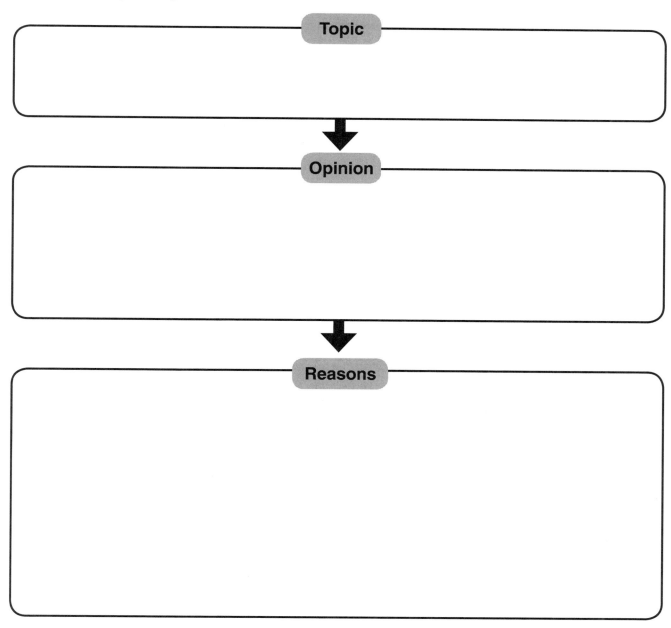

Topic

Opinion

Reasons

UNIT **9**

Safety First

Opinion

Write an opinion essay about **whether you do or do not need to be prepared for any kind of dangerous conditions or emergency.** Use information from your graphic organizer and the social studies article.

_____
Title

_____

_____

_____

_____

_____

_____

_____

_____

_____

_____

_____

_____

Evaluate Your Writing

Read about the opinion structure. Then use your essay to complete the activity below.

A text that gives an **opinion** tells how you personally feel about a subject and why you feel that way. It also includes reasons that support your opinion.

The reason for writing is clear.

My essay explained my opinion and the reasons for my opinion about:

_____

I used these opinion signal words:

_____   _____   _____

I provided reasons that support my opinion.

I included these reasons:

1. _____

2. _____

My last paragraph has a strong conclusion.

My opening sentence for the last paragraph is:

_____

My conclusion sentence for the last paragraph is:

_____

Bioengineering

Lesson Objectives

Writing
Students use information from the technology article to write an opinion essay.

Vocabulary
Students learn content vocabulary words and use those words to write about whether using bioengineering is or is not a good idea.

Content Knowledge
Students learn how Japanese engineers used biomimicry when creating their trains.

Essential Understanding
Students understand that people can benefit from studying nature when they need to create a new technology or improve upon an existing one.

Prepare the Unit

Reproduce and distribute one copy for each student.

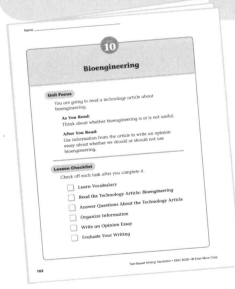

1 **Unit Focus and Lesson Checklist**

Distribute one unit to each student and direct students' attention to the Unit Focus and Lesson Checklist. Tell them they will be able to refer to the focus of the unit as needed while working on the lessons. Instruct students to check off each task on the checklist after they complete it.

Read aloud the focus statements, and verify that students understand their purpose for reading. Ask:

- *What are we going to read about?* (bioengineering)

- *What are you going to learn about it?* (whether it is or is not useful)

- *What are you going to write based on this article?* (an opinion essay)

CCSS: **W** 6.2, 6.4, 6.9   **RIT** 6.1, 6.4, 6.10

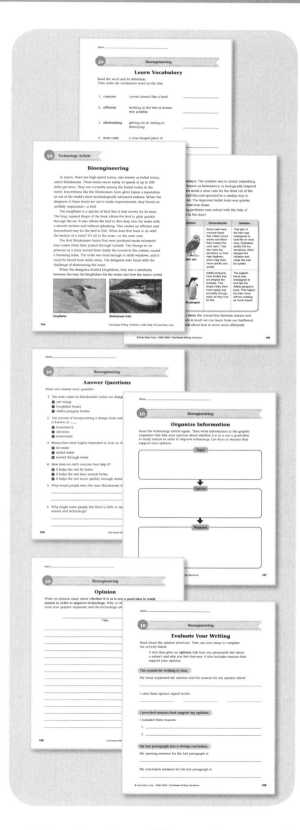

2 **Learn Vocabulary**

Read aloud each content vocabulary word and have students repeat. Then read aloud and discuss the definitions. Explain that students will have a better understanding of the words after they read the technology article. Have students write the vocabulary words on the provided lines.

3 **Read the Technology Article:** *Bioengineering*

Read aloud the technology article as students follow along silently. Then have students reread the article independently or in small groups.

4 **Answer Questions About the Technology Article**

To ensure reading comprehension, have students answer the text-dependent questions. Review the answers together.

5 **Organize Information**

Explain to students that they will use an opinion graphic organizer to help them plan their essays. Guide students in using the text to complete the organizer.

6 **Write an Opinion Essay**

Have students complete the writing assignment independently, with a partner, or in small groups.

Remind students that an opinion essay:

• tells how you feel about something,

• tells why you feel that way, and

• includes signal words: *I feel, I think, to me, I like, I agree that; I don't like, I disagree that.*

7 **Evaluate Your Writing**

Explain that students will evaluate their writing to ensure that they have produced well-written essays that follow the opinion structure.

Name _____

Bioengineering

Unit Focus

You are going to read a technology article about bioengineering.

As You Read:

Think about whether bioengineering is or is not useful.

After You Read:

Use information from the article to write an opinion essay about whether we should or should not use bioengineering.

Lesson Checklist

Check off each task after you complete it.

- [ ] **Learn Vocabulary**
- [ ] **Read the Technology Article:** *Bioengineering*
- [ ] **Answer Questions About the Technology Article**
- [ ] **Organize Information**
- [ ] **Write an Opinion Essay**
- [ ] **Evaluate Your Writing**

Text-Based Writing: Nonfiction • EMC 6036 • © Evan-Moor Corp.

UNIT
10

Learn Vocabulary

Read the word and its definition.
Then write the vocabulary word on the line.

1. **concave**   curved inward like a bowl   _____

2. **efficient**   working in the best or fastest way possible   _____

3. **eliminating**   getting rid of; ending or destroying   _____

4. **nose cone**   a cone-shaped piece of equipment on the front of a machine   _____

5. **rattle**   to make short, rapid knocking sounds, usually by shaking   _____

6. **reputation**   goodness or badness in relation to one's character or business   _____

7. **serrations**   a series of sharp saw-like notches, such as on the blade of a knife   _____

Bioengineering

In Japan, there are high-speed trains, also known as bullet trains, called Shinkansen. These trains move safely at speeds of up to 200 miles per hour. They are currently among the fastest trains in the world. Innovations like the Shinkansen have given Japan a reputation as one of the world's most technologically advanced nations. When the designers of these trains set out to make improvements, they found an unlikely inspiration—a bird.

The kingfisher is a species of bird that is best known for its beak. The long, tapered shape of the beak allows the bird to glide quickly through the air. It also allows the bird to dive deep into the water with a smooth motion and without splashing. This creates an efficient and streamlined way for the bird to fish. What does that have to do with the motion of a train? It's all in the nose—or the nose cone.

The first Shinkansen trains that were produced made extremely loud noises when they passed through tunnels. The change in air pressure as a train moved from inside the tunnel to the outside caused a booming noise. The noise was loud enough to rattle windows, and it could be heard from miles away. The designers were faced with the challenge of eliminating the noise.

When the designers studied kingfishers, they saw a similarity between the way the kingfishers hit the water and how the trains exited

Kingfisher

Shinkansen train

tunnels—with a lot of pressure. The solution was to mimic something found in nature. This is known as biomimicry, or biologically inspired engineering. The designers made a nose cone for the front car of the train. The nose cone looked like and operated in a similar way to a kingfisher's pointed beak. The improved bullet train was quieter, used less energy, and moved even faster.

Two other engineering problems were solved with the help of biomimicry, as indicated in the chart.

Problem	Animal	Characteristic	Solution
Part of the train vibrated loudly and made an extremely loud noise.	**Barn owl**	Some owls have concave faces that collect sound waves and direct them toward the owls' ears. They also have tiny serrations on their main feathers, which help them move quickly and quietly.	That part of the train was redesigned to look like an owl's wing. Engineers added the tiny serrations, which stopped the vibration and made the train far quieter.
A support frame on the train resisted wind, which created a lot of noise.	**Adélie penguin**	Adélie penguins have bodies that are shaped like footballs. This shape helps them move easily and smoothly through water as they hunt for fish.	The support frame was redesigned to look like the Adélie penguin's body. This helped the train move without creating as much sound.

People do not always make the connection between nature and technology. However, there is much we can learn from our feathered, winged, and finned friends about how to move more efficiently throughout the world.

Answer Questions

Read and answer each question.

1. The nose cones on Shinkansen trains are designed to look like ____.
   Ⓐ owl wings
   Ⓑ kingfisher beaks
   Ⓒ Adélie penguin bodies

2. The process of incorporating a design from nature into technology is known as ____.
   Ⓐ biomimicry
   Ⓑ serration
   Ⓒ innovation

3. Researchers were highly interested in how an Adélie penguin's body ____.
   Ⓐ hit water
   Ⓑ exited water
   Ⓒ moved through water

4. How does an owl's concave face help it?
   Ⓐ It helps the owl fly faster.
   Ⓑ It helps the owl hear sounds better.
   Ⓒ It helps the owl move quickly through water.

5. Why would people who live near Shinkansen trains want them to be quieter?

   _____

   _____

6. Why might some people feel there is little or no connection between nature and technology?

   _____

   _____

Organize Information

Read the technology article again. Then write information in the graphic organizer that tells your opinion about whether it is or is not a good idea to study nature in order to improve technology. List facts or reasons that support your opinion.

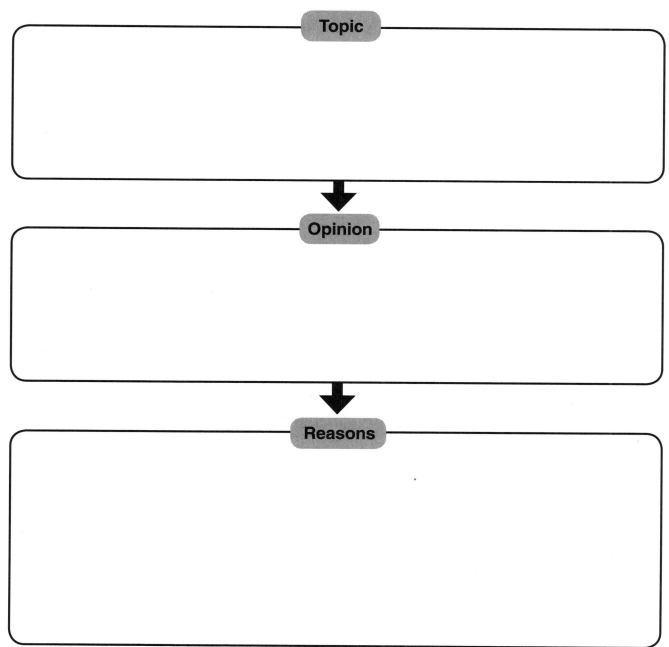

Topic

Opinion

Reasons

Name _____

Opinion

Write an opinion essay about **whether it is or is not a good idea to study nature in order to improve technology.** Why or why not? Use information from your graphic organizer and the technology article.

_____
Title

_____

_____

_____

_____

_____

_____

_____

_____

_____

_____

_____

_____

_____

UNIT 10

Evaluate Your Writing

Read about the opinion structure. Then use your essay to complete the activity below.

> A text that gives an **opinion** tells how you personally feel about a subject and why you feel that way. It also includes reasons that support your opinion.

The reason for writing is clear.

My essay explained my opinion and the reasons for my opinion about:

_____

I used these opinion signal words:

_____   _____   _____

I provided reasons that support my opinion.

I included these reasons:

1. _____

2. _____

My last paragraph has a strong conclusion.

My opening sentence for the last paragraph is:

_____

My conclusion sentence for the last paragraph is:

_____

A Penny's Worth

Lesson Objectives

Writing
Students use information from the social studies article to write an argument essay.

Vocabulary
Students learn content vocabulary words and use those words to write about whether the U.S. should or should not continue making the penny.

Content Knowledge
Students learn the history of the penny and its current value.

Essential Understanding
Students understand that even though the penny is worth very little, many people want to keep it in circulation.

Prepare the Unit

Reproduce and distribute one copy for each student.

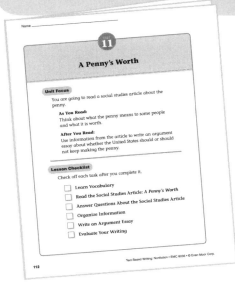

1 Unit Focus and Lesson Checklist

Distribute one unit to each student and direct students' attention to the Unit Focus and Lesson Checklist. Tell them they will be able to refer to the focus of the unit as needed while working on the lessons. Instruct students to check off each task on the checklist after they complete it.

Read aloud the focus statements, and verify that students understand their purpose for reading. Ask:

• *What are we going to read about?* (the penny)

• *What are you going to learn about it?* (whether it should or should not still be made)

• *What are you going to write based on this article?* (an argument essay)

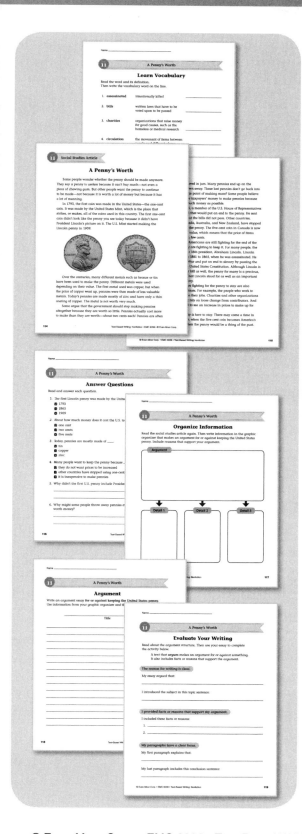

2 Learn Vocabulary

Read aloud each content vocabulary word and have students repeat. Then read aloud and discuss the definitions. Explain that students will have a better understanding of the words after they read the social studies article. Have students write the vocabulary words on the provided lines.

3 Read the Social Studies Article: *A Penny's Worth*

Read aloud the social studies article as students follow along silently. Then have students reread the article independently or in small groups.

4 Answer Questions About the Social Studies Article

To ensure reading comprehension, have students answer the text-dependent questions. Review the answers together.

5 Organize Information

Explain to students that they will use an argument graphic organizer to help them plan their essays. Guide students in using the text to complete the organizer.

6 Write an Argument Essay

Have students complete the writing assignment independently, with a partner, or in small groups.

Remind students that an argument essay:

- makes an argument for or against something,

- gives reasons or facts to support the argument, and

- includes an introductory topic sentence and a conclusion sentence at the end.

7 Evaluate Your Writing

Explain that students will evaluate their writing to ensure that they have produced well-written essays that follow the argument structure.

A Penny's Worth

Unit Focus

You are going to read a social studies article about the penny.

As You Read:

Think about what the penny means to some people and what it is worth.

After You Read:

Use information from the article to write an argument essay about whether the United States should or should not keep making the penny.

Lesson Checklist

Check off each task after you complete it.

- [ ] **Learn Vocabulary**
- [ ] **Read the Social Studies Article:** *A Penny's Worth*
- [ ] **Answer Questions About the Social Studies Article**
- [ ] **Organize Information**
- [ ] **Write an Argument Essay**
- [ ] **Evaluate Your Writing**

Learn Vocabulary

Read the word and its definition.
Then write the vocabulary word on the line.

1. **assassinated**   intentionally killed   _____

2. **bills**   written laws that have to be
voted upon to be passed   _____

3. **charities**   organizations that raise money
for good causes, such as the
homeless or medical research   _____

4. **circulation**   the movement of items between
people and different places   _____

5. **coating**   a light covering on the outer
surface   _____

6. **contributors**   people who give donations   _____

7. **denomination**   the size, form, or value
of money   _____

8. **nostalgic**   relating fondly to the past or
to history   _____

9. **worth**   having the same value as;
value in money   _____

A Penny's Worth

Some people wonder whether the penny should be made anymore. They say a penny is useless because it can't buy much—not even a piece of chewing gum. But other people want the penny to continue to be made—not because it is worth a lot of money but because it has a lot of meaning.

In 1793, the first coin was made in the United States—the one-cent coin. It was made by the United States Mint, which is the place that strikes, or makes, all of the coins used in this country. The first one-cent coin didn't look like the penny you see today because it didn't have President Lincoln's picture on it. The U.S. Mint started making the Lincoln penny in 1909.

Over the centuries, many different metals such as bronze or tin have been used to make the penny. Different metals were used depending on their value. The first metal used was copper, but when the price of copper went up, pennies were then made of less valuable metals. Today's pennies are made mostly of zinc and have only a thin coating of copper. The metal is not worth very much.

Some argue that the government should stop making pennies altogether because they are worth so little. Pennies actually cost more to make than they are worth—about two cents each! Pennies are often tossed into drawers or saved in jars. Many pennies end up on the ground or are even thrown away. These lost pennies don't go back into circulation, so what is the point of making more? Some people believe that we should not waste taxpayers' money to make pennies because we all need to save as much money as possible.

In 2001 and in 2006, a member of the U.S. House of Representatives tried to get a law passed that would put an end to the penny. He sent two bills to the House, but the bills did not pass. Other countries, however, including Canada, Australia, and New Zealand, have stopped making their version of the penny. The five-cent coin in Canada is now the coin with the lowest value, which means that the price of items may be rounded up by a few cents.

Even though many Americans are still fighting for the end of the U.S. penny, just as many are fighting to keep it. For many people, the penny is a symbol of our 16th president, Abraham Lincoln. Lincoln served as president from 1861 to 1865, when he was assassinated. He served during the Civil War and put an end to slavery by passing the 13th Amendment to the United States Constitution. Although Lincoln is shown on the five-dollar bill as well, the penny for many is a precious, nostalgic symbol of all that Lincoln stood for as well as an important part of our nation's history.

Those people who are fighting for the penny to stay are also concerned about other issues. For example, the people who work to make pennies would lose their jobs. Charities and other organizations may lose donations that rely on loose change from contributors. And many people don't want to see an increase in prices to make up for the lost cents.

So for now, the penny is here to stay. There may come a time in the near future, however, when the five-cent coin becomes America's lowest denomination. Then the penny would be a thing of the past.

Name _____

Answer Questions

Read and answer each question.

1. The first Lincoln penny was made by the United States Mint in ____.

   Ⓐ 1793

   Ⓑ 1865

   Ⓒ 1909

2. About how much money does it cost the U.S. to make each penny today?

   Ⓐ one cent

   Ⓑ two cents

   Ⓒ five cents

3. Today, pennies are mostly made of ____.

   Ⓐ tin

   Ⓑ copper

   Ⓒ zinc

4. Many people want to keep the penny because ____.

   Ⓐ they do not want prices to be increased

   Ⓑ other countries have stopped using one-cent coins

   Ⓒ it is inexpensive to make pennies

5. Why didn't the first U.S. penny include President Lincoln's image?

   _____

   _____

6. Why might some people throw away pennies even though they are worth money?

   _____

   _____

Organize Information

Read the social studies article again. Then write information in the graphic organizer that makes an argument for or against keeping the United States penny. Include reasons that support your argument.

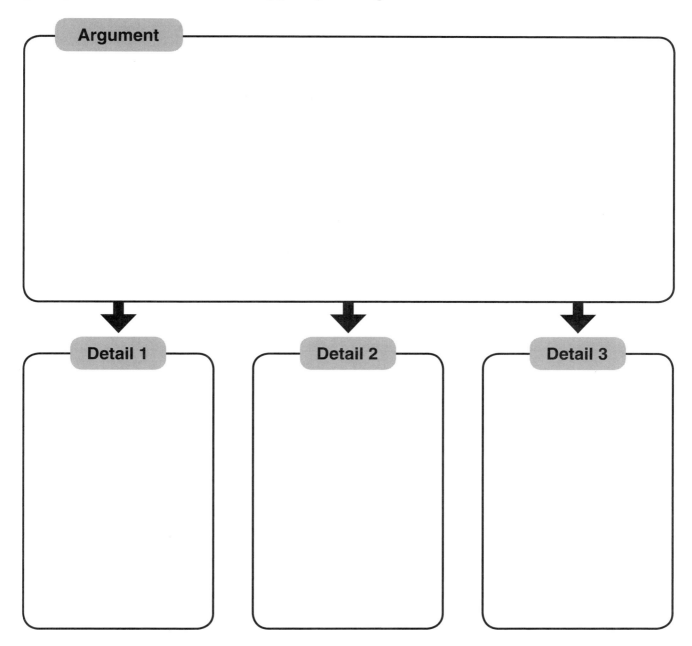

Argument

Detail 1

Detail 2

Detail 3

Name _____

Argument

Write an argument essay **for or against keeping the United States penny**. Use information from your graphic organizer and the social studies article.

_____

Title

_____

_____

_____

_____

_____

_____

_____

_____

_____

_____

_____

_____

_____

Name _____

 UNIT 11 A Penny's Worth

Evaluate Your Writing

Read about the argument structure. Then use your essay to complete the activity below.

> A text that **argues** makes an argument for or against something.
> It also includes facts or reasons that support the argument.

The reason for writing is clear.

My essay argued that:

_____

I introduced the subject in this topic sentence:

_____

I provided facts or reasons that support my argument.

I included these facts or reasons:

1. _____

2. _____

My paragraphs have a clear focus.

My first paragraph explains that:

_____

My last paragraph includes this conclusion sentence:

_____

The Science of Flavor

Lesson Objectives

Writing
Students use information from the science article to write an argument essay.

Vocabulary
Students learn content vocabulary words and use those words to write an argument for or against artificial food flavoring.

Content Knowledge
Students learn about the history of preserved food and the need for food flavorists.

Essential Understanding
Students understand that without flavorists, our food would be much different than it is today.

Prepare the Unit

Reproduce and distribute one copy for each student.

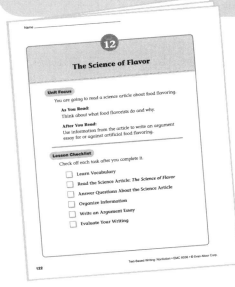

1 Unit Focus and Lesson Checklist

Distribute one unit to each student and direct students' attention to the Unit Focus and Lesson Checklist. Tell them they will be able to refer to the focus of the unit as needed while working on the lessons. Instruct students to check off each task on the checklist after they complete it.

Read aloud the focus statements, and verify that students understand their purpose for reading. Ask:

• *What are we going to read about?* (food flavoring)

• *What are you going to learn about it?* (what food flavorists do and why)

• *What are you going to write based on this article?* (an argument essay)

CCSS: W 6.2, 6.4, 6.9   RIT 6.1, 6.4, 6.10

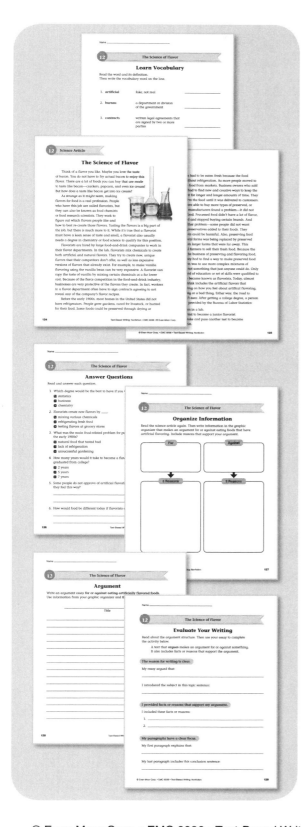

2 Learn Vocabulary

Read aloud each content vocabulary word and have students repeat. Then read aloud and discuss the definitions. Explain that students will have a better understanding of the words after they read the science article. Have students write the vocabulary words on the provided lines.

3 Read the Science Article: *The Science of Flavor*

Read aloud the science article as students follow along silently. Then have students reread the article independently or in small groups.

4 Answer Questions About the Science Article

To ensure reading comprehension, have students answer the text-dependent questions. Review the answers together.

5 Organize Information

Explain to students that they will use an argument graphic organizer to help them plan their essays. Guide students in using the text to complete the organizer.

6 Write an Argument Essay

Have students complete the writing assignment independently, with a partner, or in small groups.

Remind students that an argument essay:

- makes an argument for or against something,

- gives reasons or facts to support the argument, and

- includes an introductory topic sentence and a conclusion sentence at the end.

7 Evaluate Your Writing

Explain that students will evaluate their writing to ensure that they have produced well-written essays that follow the argument structure.

Name _____

UNIT
12

The Science of Flavor

Unit Focus

You are going to read a science article about food flavoring.

As You Read:

Think about what food flavorists do and why.

After You Read:

Use information from the article to write an argument essay for or against artificial food flavoring.

Lesson Checklist

Check off each task after you complete it.

- [ ] **Learn Vocabulary**
- [ ] **Read the Science Article:** *The Science of Flavor*
- [ ] **Answer Questions About the Science Article**
- [ ] **Organize Information**
- [ ] **Write an Argument Essay**
- [ ] **Evaluate Your Writing**

Learn Vocabulary

Read the word and its definition.
Then write the vocabulary word on the line.

1. **artificial**   fake; not real   _____

2. **bureau**   a department or division
of the government   _____

3. **contracts**   written legal agreements that
are signed by two or more
parties   _____

4. **keen**   very good; excellent   _____

5. **manufacturers**   companies that make goods
to sell to businesses or people   _____

6. **preserved**   kept from spoiling or rotting;
saved for future use   _____

7. **processed food**   food that has been modified
to last longer or taste better;
food that is not natural   _____

8. **qualify**   to be able to do something
as a result of schooling or
training   _____

The Science of Flavor

Think of a flavor you like. Maybe you love the taste of bacon. You do not have to fry actual bacon to enjoy this flavor. There are a lot of foods you can buy that are made to taste like bacon—crackers, popcorn, and even ice cream! But how does a taste like bacon get into ice cream?

As strange as it might seem, making flavors for food is a real profession. People who have this job are called flavorists, but they can also be known as food chemists or food research scientists. They work to figure out which flavors people like and

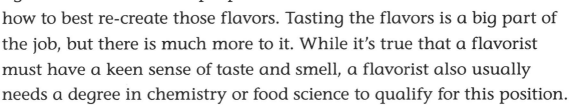

how to best re-create those flavors. Tasting the flavors is a big part of the job, but there is much more to it. While it's true that a flavorist must have a keen sense of taste and smell, a flavorist also usually needs a degree in chemistry or food science to qualify for this position.

Flavorists are hired by large food-and-drink companies to work in their flavor departments. In the lab, flavorists mix chemicals to create both artificial and natural flavors. They try to create new, unique flavors that their competitors don't offer, as well as less expensive versions of flavors that already exist. For example, to make vanilla flavoring using the vanilla bean can be very expensive. A flavorist can copy the taste of vanilla by mixing certain chemicals at a far lower cost. Because of the fierce competition in the food-and-drink industry, businesses are very protective of the flavors they create. In fact, workers in a flavor department often have to sign contracts agreeing to not reveal any of the company's flavor recipes.

Before the early 1900s, most homes in the United States did not have refrigerators. People grew gardens, cared for livestock, or hunted for their food. Some foods could be preserved through drying or canning, but other foods had to be eaten fresh because the food couldn't be preserved without refrigeration. As more people moved to cities, they bought more food from markets. Business owners who sold the food to the markets had to find new and creative ways to keep the food fresh and safe to eat for longer and longer amounts of time. They used chemicals to preserve the food until it was delivered to customers.

Over time, people were able to buy more types of preserved, or processed, food, but the manufacturers found a problem—it did not taste the same as fresh food. Processed food didn't have a lot of flavor, so customers complained and stopped buying certain brands. And manufacturers had another problem—some people did not want artificial flavoring and preservatives added to their foods. They believed that preservatives could be harmful. Also, preserving food meant that food from local farms was being replaced by preserved fruits and vegetables from larger farms that were far away. This made it difficult for local farmers to sell their fresh food. Because the manufacturers were in the business of preserving and flavoring food, not selling fresh food, they had to find a way to make preserved food taste better. Their solution was to use more complex mixtures of chemicals. But this was not something that just anyone could do. Only people with a certain kind of education or set of skills were qualified to do the job. Those people became known as flavorists. Today, almost everything we eat and drink includes the artificial flavors that flavorists make. Depending on how you feel about artifical flavoring, this could be a good thing or a bad thing. Either way, the road to becoming a flavorist isn't easy. After getting a college degree, a person would follow these steps provided by the Bureau of Labor Statistics:

1 Train for five years in a lab.

2 Take and pass a test to become a junior flavorist.

3 After two years, take and pass another test to become an official flavorist.

Name _____

Answer Questions

Read and answer each question.

1. Which degree would be the best to have if you wanted to be a flavorist?
   Ⓐ statistics
   Ⓑ business
   Ⓒ chemistry

2. Flavorists create new flavors by ____.
   Ⓐ mixing various chemicals
   Ⓑ refrigerating fresh food
   Ⓒ testing flavors at grocery stores

3. What was the main food-related problem for people who lived before the early 1900s?
   Ⓐ natural food that tasted bad
   Ⓑ lack of refrigeration
   Ⓒ unsuccessful gardening

4. How many years would it take to become a flavorist after you've graduated from college?
   Ⓐ 2 years
   Ⓑ 5 years
   Ⓒ 7 years

5. Some people do not approve of artificial flavoring. Why do you think they feel this way?

   _____

   _____

6. How would food be different today if flavorists did not exist?

   _____

   _____

Name _____

Organize Information

Read the science article again. Then write information in the graphic organizer that makes an argument for or against eating foods that have artificial flavoring. Include reasons that support your argument.

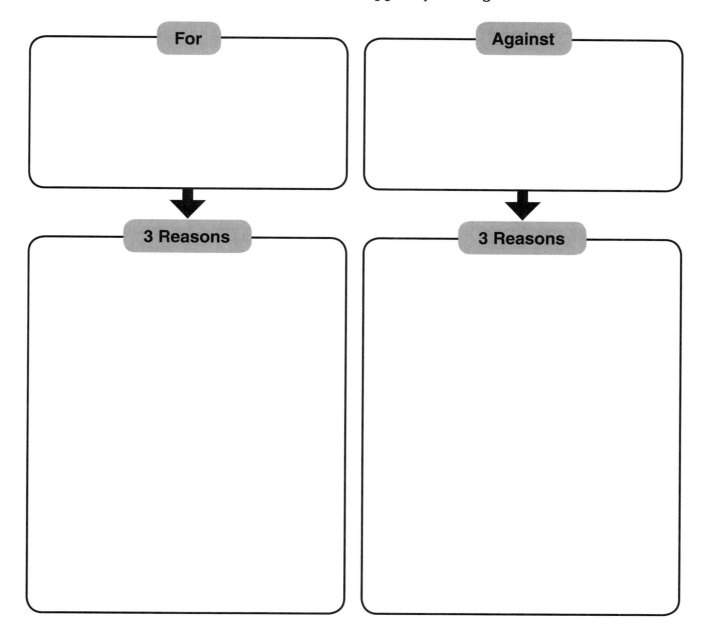

For

Against

3 Reasons

3 Reasons

Name _____

Argument

Write an argument essay **for or against eating artificially flavored foods**. Use information from your graphic organizer and the science article.

_____
Title

_____

_____

_____

_____

_____

_____

_____

_____

_____

_____

_____

_____

UNIT 12

Evaluate Your Writing

Read about the argument structure. Then use your essay to complete the activity below.

> A text that **argues** makes an argument for or against something. It also includes facts or reasons that support the argument.

The reason for writing is clear.

My essay argued that:

_____

_____

I introduced the subject in this topic sentence:

_____

_____

I provided facts or reasons that support my argument.

I included these facts or reasons:

1. _____

2. _____

My paragraphs have a clear focus.

My first paragraph explains that:

_____

_____

My last paragraph includes this conclusion sentence:

_____

_____

Answer Key

Unit 1

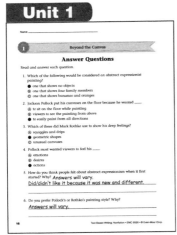

Beyond the Canvas

Answer Questions

Read and answer each question.

1. Which of the following would be considered an abstract expressionist painting?
   Ⓐ one that shows no objects
   Ⓑ one that shows four family members
   Ⓒ one that shows bananas and oranges

2. Jackson Pollock put his canvases on the floor because he wanted ____.
   Ⓐ to sit on the floor while painting
   Ⓑ viewers to see the painting from above
   Ⓒ to easily paint from all directions

3. Which of these did Mark Rothko use to show his deep feelings?
   Ⓐ squiggles and drips
   Ⓑ geometric shapes
   Ⓒ unusual canvases

4. Pollock most wanted viewers to feel his ____.
   Ⓐ emotions
   Ⓑ desires
   Ⓒ actions

5. How do you think people felt about abstract expressionism when it first started? Why? Answers will vary.
   Did/didn't like it because it was new and different.

6. Do you prefer Pollock's or Rothko's painting style? Why?
   Answers will vary.

TE Page 16 / SB Page 8

Beyond the Canvas

Organize Information

Read the art article again. Then write information in the Venn diagram that tells how the styles and paintings of Jackson Pollock and Mark Rothko are alike and different.

Jackson Pollock
used many gallons of paint, moved all around the painting, wanted to show action, used drips and squiggles

Both
abstract expressionists, showed feelings, didn't show real-life things, used large canvases, used bold colors, wanted to connect with viewers

used color fields, wanted to show feelings, used geometric shapes

Mark Rothko

TE Page 17 / SB Page 9

Unit 2

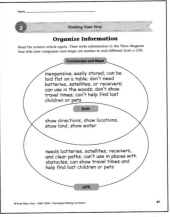

Finding Your Way

Answer Questions

Read and answer each question.

1. Which of the following does a GPS need in order to function properly?
   Ⓐ a table on which to study it
   Ⓑ exposure to sea currents
   Ⓒ a clear path to satellites

2. The function of a compass is to show ____.
   Ⓐ directions
   Ⓑ landmasses
   Ⓒ waterways

3. Some people prefer compasses and maps because they do not require ____.
   Ⓐ reading
   Ⓑ understanding directions
   Ⓒ batteries

4. A GPS would work better than a standard map for ____.
   Ⓐ seeing the shapes of various countries
   Ⓑ locating a lost child at a shopping center
   Ⓒ finding your route through an underground cave

5. How did early explorers use the sun and the stars to travel? Explain.
   They looked at their positions and used them like a map.

6. The article ends with a question. What is your answer? Why?
   Answers will vary.

TE Page 26 / SB Page 16

Finding Your Way

Organize Information

Read the science article again. Then write information in the Venn diagram that tells how compasses and maps are similar to and different from a GPS.

Compasses and Maps
inexpensive; easily stored; can be laid flat on a table; don't need batteries, satellites, or receivers; can use in the woods; don't show travel times; can't help find lost children or pets

Both
show directions, show locations, show land, show water

needs batteries, satellites, receivers, and clear paths; can't use in places with obstacles; can show travel times and help find lost children or pets

GPS

TE Page 27 / SB Page 17

Unit 3

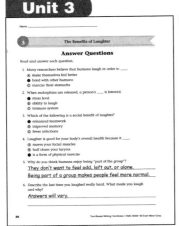

The Benefits of Laughter

Answer Questions

Read and answer each question.

1. Many researchers believe that humans laugh in order to ____.
   Ⓐ make themselves feel better
   Ⓑ bond with other humans
   Ⓒ exercise their stomachs

2. When endorphins are released, a person's ____ is lowered.
   Ⓐ stress level
   Ⓑ ability to laugh
   Ⓒ immune system

3. Which of the following is a social benefit of laughter?
   Ⓐ enhanced teamwork
   Ⓑ improved memory
   Ⓒ fewer infections

4. Laughter is good for your body's overall health because it ____.
   Ⓐ moves your facial muscles
   Ⓑ half closes your larynx
   Ⓒ is a form of physical exercise

5. Why do you think humans enjoy being "part of the group"?
   They don't want to feel odd, left out, or alone.
   Being part of a group makes people feel more normal.

6. Describe the last time you laughed really hard. What made you laugh and why?
   Answers will vary.

TE Page 36 / SB Page 24

The Benefits of Laughter

Organize Information

Read the health article again. Then write information in the graphic organizer that tells the causes and effects of laughter.

Answers may vary.

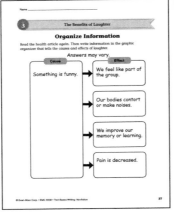

Cause	Effect
Something is funny.	We feel like part of the group.
	Our bodies contort or make noises.
	We improve our memory or learning.
	Pain is decreased.

TE Page 37 / SB Page 25

Unit 4

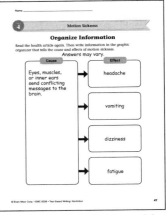

Motion Sickness

Answer Questions

Read and answer each question.

1. Motion sickness occurs when your eyes and your ____ send conflicting messages to your brain.
   Ⓐ stomach
   Ⓑ inner ears
   Ⓒ legs

2. You can feel motion sickness if you are lacking a sense of ____.
   Ⓐ hearing
   Ⓑ balance
   Ⓒ strength

3. Which of the following is least likely to cause motion sickness?
   Ⓐ walking on a trail
   Ⓑ riding on a bus
   Ⓒ flying in an airplane

4. Which of these could help if you have motion sickness?
   Ⓐ reading a book
   Ⓑ playing a video game
   Ⓒ breathing some fresh air

5. What might cause an astronaut to get spacesick?
   An astronaut is floating, not balanced on the ground.
   So his or her eyes, inner ears, and muscles are sending mixed signals to the brain.

6. Do you think closing your eyes might help you if you have motion sickness? Why or why not? Answers may vary.
   Yes, closing your eyes stops messages about what you are seeing from going to your brain.

TE Page 46 / SB Page 32

Motion Sickness

Organize Information

Read the health article again. Then write information in the graphic organizer that tells the cause and effects of motion sickness.

Answers may vary.

Cause	Effect
Eyes, muscles, or inner ears send conflicting messages to the brain.	headache
	vomiting
	dizziness
	fatigue

TE Page 47 / SB Page 33

Unit 5

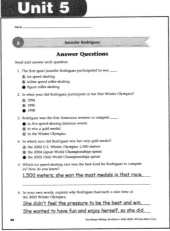

Jennifer Rodriguez

Answer Questions

Read and answer each question.

1. The first sport Jennifer Rodriguez participated in was ____.
   Ⓐ ice speed skating
   Ⓑ inline speed roller-skating
   Ⓒ figure roller-skating

2. In what year did Rodriguez participate in her first Winter Olympics?
   Ⓐ 1994
   Ⓑ 1996
   Ⓒ 1998

3. Rodriguez was the first American woman to compete ____.
   Ⓐ in five speed-skating distance events
   Ⓑ to win a gold medal
   Ⓒ in the Winter Olympics

4. In which race did Rodriguez win her only gold medal?
   Ⓐ the 2002 U.S. Winter Olympics 1,500 meters
   Ⓑ the 2004 Japan World Championships sprint
   Ⓒ the 2005 Utah World Championships sprint

5. Which ice speed-skating race was the best race for Rodriguez to compete in? How do you know?
   1,500 meters; she won the most medals in that race.

6. In your own words, explain why Rodriguez had such a nice time at the 2010 Winter Olympics.
   She didn't feel the pressure to be the best and win.
   She wanted to have fun and enjoy herself, so she did.

TE Page 56 / SB Page 40

Jennifer Rodriguez

Organize Information

Read the biography again. Then write information in the graphic organizer that lists causes and effects in Jennifer Rodriguez's life that led to her success.

Answers may vary.

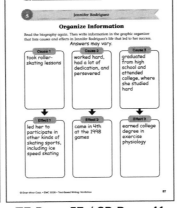

Cause 1	Cause 2	Cause 3
took roller-skating lessons	worked hard, had a lot of dedication, and persevered	graduated from high school and attended college, where she studied hard

Effect 1	Effect 2	Effect 3
led her to participate in other kinds of skating sports, including ice speed skating	came in 4th at the 1998 games	earned college degree in exercise physiology

TE Page 57 / SB Page 41

Unit 6

Fancy Fliers

Answer Questions

Read and answer each question.

1. In tropical forests, hummingbirds cannot eat from ____.
   Ⓐ passionflowers
   Ⓑ nectar feeders
   Ⓒ flowers

2. How many flowers does a typical hummingbird need to visit each day?
   Ⓐ 10 to 20
   Ⓑ 2 to 50
   Ⓒ 200 or more

3. The sword-billed hummingbird uses its long bill to get nectar from a passionflower's ____.
   Ⓐ pollen
   Ⓑ petals
   Ⓒ corolla

4. Flowers rely on hummingbirds to help the flowers ____.
   Ⓐ transport pollen
   Ⓑ stay protected from other birds
   Ⓒ produce nectar

5. What might happen if all the passionflowers died off?
   The sword-billed hummingbird might not be able to find enough food; it might go extinct, too.

6. What might happen if you tried to remove a hummingbird's sources of food? Why?
   A hummingbird might attack you because it is very territorial with its food sources.

TE Page 66 / SB Page 48

Fancy Fliers

Organize Information

Read the science article again. Then write information in the graphic organizer that explains how hummingbirds work to stay alive.

gather nectar each day

visit hundreds of flowers a day

Hummingbirds

guard their territories and food sources from other birds or insects

adapt to get food from certain flowers

TE Page 67 / SB Page 49

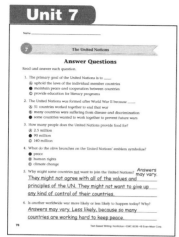

TE Page 76 / SB Page 56

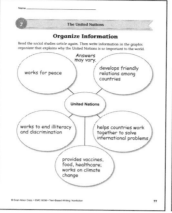

TE Page 77 / SB Page 57

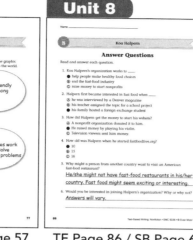

TE Page 86 / SB Page 64

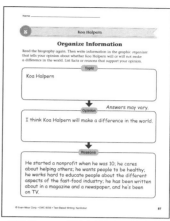

TE Page 87 / SB Page 65

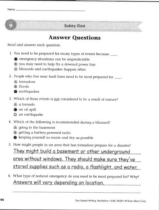

TE Page 96 / SB Page 72

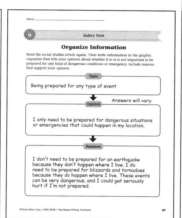

TE Page 97 / SB Page 73

TE Page 106 / SB Page 80

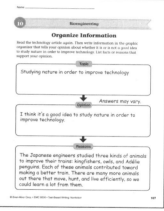

TE Page 107 / SB Page 81

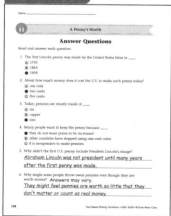

TE Page 116 / SB Page 88

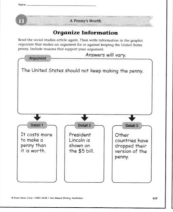

TE Page 117 / SB Page 89

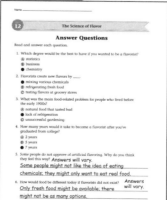

TE Page 126 / SB Page 96

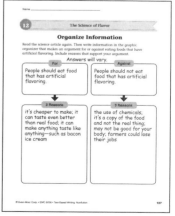

TE Page 127 / SB Page 97

Common Core Lessons

Reading Informational Text

Grade 6

SAMPLER

Social Studies Article
Text Structure: Main Idea and Details

Ancient Economies

Lesson Objective
Students will explain the main economic strategies that helped the civilizations of ancient Egypt and the Indus River prosper.

Content Knowledge
Historic information can be classified according to the type of activity or practice, including social/cultural, economic, scientific, or political. Important historic developments of past civilizations have contributed to contemporary cultures and societies.

Lesson Preparation

Reproduce and distribute one copy of the article, dictionary page, and activity pages to each student.

CCSS: RIT 6.1, 6.2, 6.3, 6.4, 6.5, 6.7 W 6.2, 6.4, 6.9.b

1 Read Aloud the Article

Read aloud *Ancient Economies*. Have students follow along silently as you read.

2 Introduce the Vocabulary

Content Vocabulary

Read aloud the Content Vocabulary words and definitions. Point out that *agriculture* contains the prefix *agri-*, which comes from a Greek word meaning "field." Explain that another word with a related prefix is *agronomy*—the science of caring for the soil and producing crops. Discuss definitions and usage as needed.

Academic Vocabulary

Next, read aloud the Academic Vocabulary words and definitions. Discuss definitions and usage as needed. Then read these context sentences from the article, emphasizing the Academic Vocabulary words:

*The civilizations of ancient Egypt and the Indus Valley prospered because of their economies and their economic **strategies**.*

*Ancient Egyptians had easy **access** to the Nile's fresh water, which allowed their agricultural efforts to **flourish**.*

*Ancient Egypt's economy also benefited from the **development** of new kinds of transportation.*

*Agriculture was important to the Indus Valley economy because it **guaranteed** that everyone had enough food to survive.*

3 Students Read the Article

Have students read the article independently, with a partner, or in small groups. After students read, guide a discussion about the article. Direct students' attention to graphic elements or visual aids.

4 Identify Information

Explain that students will locate important information in the article. After students complete the activity, allow time for a question-and-answer session.

5 Answer Questions

Encourage students to use the article to answer the questions and/or check their answers.

6 Apply Vocabulary

Have students reread the article before they complete the vocabulary activity.

7 Examine Text Structure

Read aloud the Main Idea and Details description and Signal Words. Then have students read the article again, underlining signal words in red. Then guide students in completing the activity.

8 Write About It: *Successful Economic Strategies*

Have students complete the writing activity independently or in small groups.

Name: _____

Ancient
Economies

Every society has an economic system that helps it prosper. The civilizations of ancient Egypt and the Indus Valley prospered because of their economies and their economic strategies. These included using local resources, developing new methods of transportation, and trading goods with people far away. In fact, their economic strategies are still useful in our modern world.

Egypt is located in the northeast corner of Africa. The civilization of ancient Egypt was near both the Nile River and the Mediterranean Sea. Ancient Egyptians had easy access to the Nile's fresh water, which allowed their agricultural efforts to flourish.

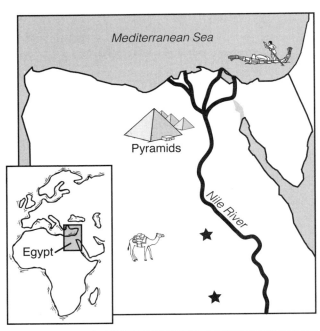

★ Locations where ancient Egyptians built monuments

They created an advanced irrigation system to water the fruits, vegetables, and grains that they grew. They also made good use of the Nile by catching fish. In addition to having locally grown food—a key element in their survival and growth—ancient Egyptians had easy access to building materials. They used local stone to build monuments, temples, tombs, and pyramids. Most ancient Egyptians lived in houses made of dry mud, which was another readily available material.

Ancient Egypt's economy also benefited from the development of new kinds of transportation. For centuries, ancient Egyptians used camels and donkeys for land travel. The development of boats for water transportation allowed them to trade with people in faraway lands. Trade was beneficial for them because it allowed them to obtain valuable items that were not available locally, such as gold and ivory.

The Indus Valley civilization was located in the present-day Asian countries of Pakistan and India. Its economy was similar to the economy of ancient Egypt in many ways. The people had access to water—in this case, the Indus River and the Arabian Sea. Like the ancient Egyptians, the Indus Valley people built an advanced irrigation system so they could use fresh water from the river to grow fruits, vegetables, and grains. Agriculture was important to the Indus Valley economy because it guaranteed that everyone had enough food to survive. Being near water also inspired the Indus Valley people to build boats, which allowed them to travel to distant lands to trade goods. Through trade, the people obtained gold, copper, livestock, and precious stones such as turquoise. These goods could only be acquired through trade with other lands.

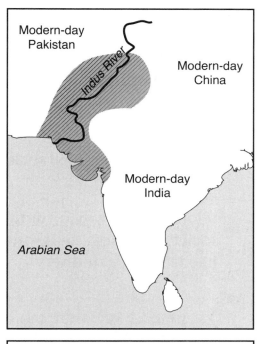

Indus Valley Civilization

The economic systems of ancient civilizations formed a model for modern economies. Think about how your own society's economy works. Your city and state probably make use of resources that are readily available in your location. For example, you may live in an area with rich soil that is well suited for agriculture. If you live in a coastal area, seafood is most likely a plentiful resource. The businesses involved in using these resources probably transport many of their goods to other states and countries. These same businesses probably bring in many other goods that cannot be produced locally. These strategies for economic success have been around since the civilizations of ancient Egypt and the Indus Valley, and they'll likely continue to be used in the future.

Dictionary

....

Content Vocabulary

agriculture
the science or profession
of farming

civilizations
advanced, organized societies

economic
related to the way a country or
society produces, sells, and buys
needed goods and services

irrigation
the practice of watering land
to promote plant growth

resources
supplies of things that are useful
or valuable to people

Academic Vocabulary

strategies
careful plans or methods for
achieving goals or solving
problems

access
a way of getting to a place
or getting a resource

flourish
to be successful and grow

development
the process of creating something
over a period of time

guaranteed
promised or made certain

Write a sentence that includes at least one vocabulary word.

_____

_____

_____

Identify Information

Check the box after you complete each task.

		Completed
✏️	Highlight the sentence in the first paragraph that mentions three economic strategies used by the civilizations of ancient Egypt and the Indus Valley.	☐
—	Underline the sentences that tell the locations of ancient Egypt and the Indus Valley.	☐
☐	Draw boxes around the bodies of water that are near each of the civilizations mentioned in the article.	☐
~	Draw a squiggly line under phrases that tell how ancient Egyptians and the Indus Valley people used fresh water.	☐
[ ]	Put brackets around sentences that tell what types of food were eaten by the people of the two civilizations.	☐
▲	Put a triangle next to things that the ancient Egyptians built out of local materials.	☐
=	Double underline the kinds of transportation used by each civilization.	☐
★	Put a star by each item or material that had trade value for either civilization.	☐
✔	Put a check mark next to the sentences that mention examples of local resources in modern economies.	☐
?	Put a question mark beside any words or sentences you don't understand.	☐

Answer Questions

Use information from the article to answer each question.

1. Closeness to _____ helped the ancient Egyptians and the Indus Valley people develop advanced civilizations.
   - Ⓐ islands
   - Ⓑ deserts
   - Ⓒ mountains
   - Ⓓ water

2. According to the article, _____ was a feature of ancient economies.
   - Ⓐ selling property
   - Ⓑ trade with other societies
   - Ⓒ having a bank account
   - Ⓓ factory labor

3. _____ were a form of transportation used by both the ancient Egyptians and the Indus Valley people.
   - Ⓐ Camels
   - Ⓑ Donkeys
   - Ⓒ Boats
   - Ⓓ Wagons

4. What is the most likely reason that many ancient Egyptians lived in houses made of dry mud?

   _____

   _____

5. Why was it important for the civilizations of ancient Egypt and the Indus Valley to develop advanced irrigation methods?

   _____

   _____

Reading Informational Text • EMC 3206 • © Evan-Moor Corp.

Name: _____

Apply Vocabulary

Use a word from the word box to complete each sentence.

Word Box

economic	civilizations	access	flourish
guaranteed	agriculture	irrigation	strategies
development	resources		

1. Ancient Egyptians used water from the Nile River for _____.

2. The _____ of water transportation allowed the ancient Egyptians and the Indus Valley people to trade with faraway lands.

3. Because of their success with _____, the ancient Egyptians had a steady food supply.

4. The people of the Indus Valley traded for gold and copper because those two _____ weren't available locally.

5. Modern-day societies use many of the same _____ as societies of long ago.

6. Using local resources is an _____ practice that is still used today.

7. Ancient Egyptians had _____ to different building materials.

8. Growing their food _____ that ancient peoples could survive.

9. Early _____ teach us a lot about how societies can prosper.

10. A civilization can _____ using wise economic strategies.

Name: _____

Main Idea and Details

A text that has a **main idea and details** structure mentions the major ideas with supporting details in any order. The main idea is usually the topic sentence of a paragraph. Signal words indicate supporting details.

Authors use these signal words to create a **main idea and details** structure:

Signal Words

another	such as	in this case	as well as
for instance	also	including	to begin with
for example	in addition	to illustrate	besides

1. The topic sentence in the first paragraph tells us that the main idea of the article is:

   _____

   _____

2. For each ancient economy discussed in the article, list one local resource and one detail about it.

   a. _____

   _____

   b. _____

   _____

3. Write two sentences from the article that use **main idea and details** signal words.

   a. _____

   _____

   b. _____

   _____

Reading Informational Text • EMC 3206 • © Evan-Moor Corp.

Name: _____

Write About It

Explain the main economic strategies that helped the civilizations of ancient Egypt and the Indus Valley prosper. Include details from the article in your explanation.

Successful Economic Strategies

_____

_____

_____

_____

_____

_____

_____

_____

_____

_____

_____

_____

_____

_____

_____

_____

_____